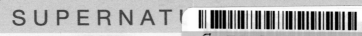

# SUPERNAT...

P9-CRD-064

3 5674 03002221 7

# Get The Scoop

## Hollywood Hunks
# BURNING
## UP THE
# SILVER
# SCREEN

## Secrets of the Stars

**an unauthorized biography about the boys of the Twilight Saga**
**BY RONNY BLOOM**

*PSS!*
Price Stern Sloan

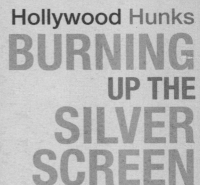

MAR 1 0

PRICE STERN SLOAN
Published by the Penguin Group
Penguin Group (USA) Inc., 375 Hudson Street, New York, New York 10014, USA
Penguin Group (Canada), 90 Eglinton Avenue East, Suite 700, Toronto, Ontario M4P
2Y3, Canada (a division of Pearson Penguin Canada Inc.)
Penguin Books Ltd., 80 Strand, London WC2R 0RL, England
Penguin Group Ireland, 25 St. Stephen's Green, Dublin 2, Ireland
(a division of Penguin Books Ltd.)
Penguin Group (Australia), 250 Camberwell Road,
Camberwell, Victoria 3124, Australia
(a division of Pearson Australia Group Pty. Ltd.)
Penguin Books India Pvt. Ltd., 11 Community Centre, Panchsheel Park,
New Delhi—110 017, India
Penguin Group (NZ), 67 Apollo Drive, Rosedale, North Shore 0632, New Zealand
(a division of Pearson New Zealand Ltd.)
Penguin Books (South Africa) (Pty.) Ltd., 24 Sturdee Avenue, Rosebank,
Johannesburg 2196, South Africa

Penguin Books Ltd., Registered Offices: 80 Strand, London WC2R 0RL, England

Photo credits: Cover: Alberto E. Rodriguez/Getty Images; Insert photos: first page
courtesy of Frank Micelotta/Getty Images; second page courtesy of Charley
Gallay/WireImage; Jeff Vespa/WireImage; third page courtesy of Alexandra
Wyman/WireImage; Chris Hatcher/Prphotos.com; fourth page courtesy of
Kevin Winter/Getty Images; Kevin Mazur/WireImage.

Library of Congress Control Number: 2009027144

ISBN 978-0-8431-9967-3    10 9 8 7 6 5 4 3 2 1

# CONTENTS

# INTRODUCTION

Actors mill about on the set, mixing with the crew. Everyone is in high spirits, and why not? They're in the midst of filming *New Moon*, the sequel to 2008's smash hit *Twilight*. That movie was adapted from the first book in Stephenie Meyer's best-selling series of the same name, and *New Moon* is adapted from the second book. The first movie was wildly popular, and everyone (especially the lead actors) has high hopes that the second will delight fans just as much.

While they're waiting for their cues, the actors hang out together, talking and laughing. They all bonded while making the first movie, and now they're close friends. Muscular, blond Kellan Lutz jokes with wiry Jackson Rathbone, and together the pair teases Robert Pattinson. Kellan, Jackson, and Robert play brothers who also happen to be vampires and, as a result, the three boys spend a lot of time together both on-screen and off. But they don't ignore Taylor Lautner, despite the fact that his character, Jacob Black, is a werewolf and a hereditary enemy to the vamps.

Finally the director is ready to shoot the next scene, which involves Taylor and Kristen Stewart, whose character, Bella, is the human love interest of both Jacob and Robert's characters. The other leading men shout encouragement as Taylor heads toward the cameras, and in reply he smiles and waves good-naturedly. Taylor had to fight to keep his role in this movie, due to significant changes in Jacob's character between the first installment of the series and the second, and the other actors were all rooting for him the entire time. Despite the fact that they're sworn mortal enemies on-screen, when the camera stops, the four boys of *Twilight* are all good friends.

# CHAPTER 1
# Bound by *Twilight*

Two young men glare at each other from their respective vehicles, and the differences between them couldn't be more pronounced. One boy has a dark complexion and the glossy, black hair of a Native American, and is wearing casual, comfortable work clothes as battered but as solid as his truck. The other is pale as milk, perfectly coiffed, in the effortlessly elegant clothes of the wealthy, and looks completely comfortable behind the wheel of his sleek, expensive sports car. The hostility between them is visible, and does not go unnoticed by the young lady in the sports car's passenger seat. Then the car and the truck move apart, and the moment ends—the cameras stop rolling, and the boys who seem to hate each other so much on-screen go back to being friends.

After the shot is captured, everyone looks at the

dailies (the footage that was filmed that day) and admires the scene. It's a perfect capture of the rivalry between Jacob Black and Edward Cullen, werewolf and vampire. Both Taylor Lautner, who plays Jacob, and Robert Pattinson, who plays Edward, are pleased with the scene, and they congratulate each other on a job well done. Kellan Lutz and Jackson Rathbone, who play Edward's vampire foster brothers, join in the good cheer. There are no bad feelings between these boys off-camera, that's for sure! Far from it—the four actors have bonded together while working on *Twilight*. They've also become friends with Kristen Stewart, who plays the movie's main human character, Bella (who is also the object of Jacob and Edward's mutual interest); Ashley Greene, who plays the Cullens' vampire foster-sister Alice; and Nikki Reed, who plays their foster-sister Rosalie. The seven youngsters, along with actor Peter Facinelli as the vampire patriarch, Dr. Carlisle Cullen, and Billy Burke as Bella's father, Sheriff Charlie Swan, form the central cast of the movie. But for legions of female fans worldwide, *Twilight* is all about the four boys.

All four of the male stars are used to the kind of attention that comes along with leading roles in films. Jackson, Kellan, Robert, and Taylor have all been acting for years, and have all attracted a fair amount of interest from moviegoers, particularly girls. Even so, none of them were prepared for the fervor that would surround them once they were announced as part of *Twilight*'s cast. The Twilight book series is an international phenomenon, with more than 10 million copies sold worldwide, and fans get every bit as excited about the books as girls did about the Beatles back in the day. There are literally thousands of websites devoted to the books and films, and all sorts of merchandise as well. It was almost a given that whomever got cast in the movie would be catapulted to instant celebrity status.

And who better than these four? They're all very different—tall, muscular Kellan; wiry, dark-haired Jackson; stoic, strong-jawed Robert; and baby-faced, friendly Taylor—but all were already considered teen heartthrobs. Now their faces can be seen everywhere, from the pages of the most popular magazines to all the hottest red carpet events, and the series hasn't even finished filming yet!

So who are these four young men, really? How did they get their starts? What are they like? How are they handling their newfound fame, and what else is in store for them? We have the answers! If you're interested—and you know you are—read on to find out!

# CHAPTER 2
# The Fifth Is Born First

The Rathbones have a long and proud history, particularly in oil. Back in 1921, Monroe Jackson Rathbone II had just earned a degree in chemical engineering from Lehigh University in Pennsylvania. Jersey Standard Oil offered him a job as a design and drafting engineer in their Baton Rouge, Louisiana, plant. That was no surprise, really—Rathbone Sr. had also worked for Jersey Standard, and Monroe's grandfather had worked on some of the industry's earliest refineries. But neither of those men had possessed Monroe's flair. A little over thirty years later, in 1954, Rathbone became the president of Jersey Standard. In 1960, he became its CEO. Over the next five years, he integrated Standard and one of its largest competitors, Humble Oil of Texas, into a single company and the world's largest oil producer.

That company's name was Exxon.

Monroe J. Rathbone IV continued the tradition, becoming an engineer in the oil industry. Because of his job, he and his family moved around a lot. By the time their fourth child was born on December 21, 1984, the family was living in Singapore! This was their first boy, and the Rathbones actually considered not continuing the family tradition of naming their first-born son Monroe Jackson. "My parents were going to name me Paul," Jackson revealed at a Q&A session at the *Twilight* Convention in San Francisco. "But my grandfather called my dad and gave him a tongue-lashing." So Monroe Jackson Rathbone V it was! Though *Twilight* fans just know him as Jackson, which is a little bit easier.

The Rathbones didn't stay in Singapore long. Their next stop was Indonesia. After that, they hit London, Connecticut, California, Norway, and finally Midland, Texas. That eventually became home, and it was there that Jackson really grew up.

Texas was also where Jackson first got interested in theater, in the form of a local community theater's youth actors program called the Pickwick Players—though initially it wasn't his choice to join the group!

As he told examiner.com, "My parents made me join the program because I wasn't making friends at school when our family moved to Midland, and my sister had joined the group. I started off as a tech-guy, building sets and running sound and the lighting boards . . . then I noticed the guys on stage were [the ones] getting all the girls, so . . . there you go."

Performing onstage led to another exciting discovery. "I was playing the role of 'Doody' [in the musical *Grease*] and had to play guitar for the part," Jackson told the fansite jackson-rathbone.com. "I fell in love with the guitar as soon as we met. Love at first song. Shame that the song had to be 'Those Magic Changes' from *Grease*." But despite the unfortunate song choice, Jackson had found a genuine love for music, and he has rarely been without a guitar since. He even brings his guitar, Annabelle, with him to acting auditions! As he explained to *Portrait* magazine, "I like to bring my guitar with me to auditions . . . it calms me down."

Jackson may have begun acting because he was interested in girls, but he wasn't very good at pursuing them! At least, not at first. He had his first kiss when he was thirteen. "I was dating a girl two years older than me," he recounted to *Seventeen*. "We were in a movie theater and got about thirty minutes into the movie (*Titanic*) and she made the first move. I was very shy and probably wouldn't have ever made the first move, so, well, it rocked my world." So what ultimately happened to the relationship? "We dated on and off for two years. I heard she recently got married, so I won't say her name, but she still holds a special place in my heart." Awww!

In fact, the three girls Jackson was closest to were his older sisters. Not that he let them dress him up or anything—or so he claims! "I got stuck with all the masculinity," Jackson insisted to radaronline.com. "I taught my sisters how to fight." Of course, that's not what he told *Seventeen* magazine! There he revealed, "I got my butt kicked a few times by my sisters. But I grew up so southern that my father would say, 'You take it like a man.' And I'd be like, 'Oh, what? I'm 5!'"

The Rathbones have always been a close-knit family. "We are a complete family unit," Jackson told *Seventeen*. "I couldn't function without any of them.

Our family dinners are the most amazing experiences: no one gets to finish a sentence, everyone laughs food through his/her nose at some point, and the food is DELICIOUS and ABUNDANT. Leftovers rock!" As the only boy, Jackson does get protective, too. He explained to *Seventeen* magazine, "When it comes to my sisters' boyfriends, I'm either cool with them or my sisters know that I hate them. I'm pretty blunt with them and to the point. Back in high school, there were a couple of boys my sisters had and man, I let them know I didn't like them." But did Jackson's disapproval actually make a difference? "I was pretty upfront but my dad always had it right," Jackson admitted. "Whenever my sisters brought them over to the house for the first time, he'd be teaching me how to clean the shotguns." Good to know!

Jackson's close relationship with his sisters also affected how he treated other women, especially his girlfriends! "My dad always taught me to treat my girlfriends the way I wanted my sisters to be treated by their boyfriends," he told *Seventeen*. "They always taught me a really wonderful level of respect that's not common these days."

Jackson was an active boy and an equally active teenager. He was interested in sports, and played basketball, soccer, baseball, football, and ran track. He loved music and started both a band (the early predecessor to his current group, 100 Monkeys) and a mobile DJ business. And once he'd joined the Pickwick Players, he discovered that he loved acting as well. With so many things going on, it was hard to focus, so Jackson decided to concentrate on his two favorite activities: acting and music. He applied and was accepted to the Interlochen Arts Academy, a prestigious creative arts high school in northwestern Michigan. It was hard leaving his family back in Texas, but Jackson knew if he really wanted to excel, he had to get the best education and the most rigorous training possible, and that was at Interlochen. "Basically, it's a high school for the arts," Jackson told *MediaBlvd* magazine, "and I studied acting as a major there, and that's when I really got into doing all the music as well. It's an amazing music school."

High school was an interesting study in contrasts for Jackson. On the one hand, he did really well in his classes, especially classical theater and particularly Shakespearean plays. Between his junior and senior years, he performed as Ferdinand, the young male lead in *The Tempest*, at the Southwest Shakespeare Festival. On the other hand, however, Jackson and his high school friends were a bit less . . . obedient. "My friends and I were kind of the bad kids in school, the troublemakers," Jackson told *Inked* magazine. "There were six of us who were always acting out against authority. The school administration was like, 'Stay away from those boys—they're "Lost Boys,"' so that's what everyone called us. When I was eighteen, I got a tattoo that says, 'I'm lost.'" Jackson still has that tattoo, though both the ear piercing and the tongue piercing he got in high school have long since healed over! He's still friends with the other Lost Boys as well, though one of them, Spencer Bell, succumbed unexpectedly to adrenal cancer a few years ago. In fact, Jackson's high-school roommate Ben Graupner and their friend Ben Johnson would later become instrumental in Jackson's continuing musical career.

After high school, Jackson had every intention of

continuing his training as an actor. He had applied and been accepted to the Royal Scottish Academy in Edinburgh, Scotland, as a theater major. That wasn't until the fall, however, and his summer plans were completely open. Jackson's best friend, Alex Boyd, had already moved to Los Angeles, and urged Jackson to join him out there. *Why not?* Jackson thought. It would give him more time to hang out with his buddy, and would give him some insight into the movie industry. So he packed his belongings and headed off to Hollywood for what he intended to be only one short summer. It wound up being far, far longer.

# CHAPTER 3
# Fame Comes A-Kellan

The year was 1985. The Lutzes lived in Dickinson, a nice, quiet town in North Dakota. They had plenty of space, and they needed it—they already had a three-year-old son, and they were about to have a second child! Kellan Christopher Lutz was born on March 15, and spent his early childhood in Dickinson, which calls itself the "Gateway to Theodore Roosevelt National Park." Obviously Kellan got his love of the outdoors at an early age!

When he was six, Kellan's parents divorced. It was a difficult time for the Lutz family, especially since Kellan, his mom, and his older brother, Brandon, left Dickinson and moved around for a while. "After the divorce, I had it really hard and we were scraping pennies," Kellan told *MediaBlvd* magazine. "I didn't live out of a box or anything, but poverty was around." They wound up living in several cities in the Midwest, but Kellan was an outgoing, energetic boy and made friends quickly in each new location. His blond good looks won him attention from the girls almost immediately. His first kiss was fairly early, as he tells *Seventeen*: "I was young, actually, maybe like third or fourth grade. It was during Truth or Dare between one of my guy friends and two of our girlfriends. The girls would put their lip balm on—I was obsessed with it! The flavors were chocolate, caramel, and strawberry (that one just took my breath away!)." Make a note, girls!

Acting also started early for Kellan. "My family has always been very church-oriented," he told newfaces.com, "so of course my mother always wanted to see her sons dress up, act, and sing in the church plays. The thing that was different between my other brothers and I was that I found the plays to be really fun and I really got into them."

Kellan is close with his whole family—"I loved growing up with such a big family filled with boys," he told the fansite twilightmoms.com. "I really don't know what I would have done if I was an only child." But he and Brandon (the only one of his older brothers who has the same father as Kellan) share a special bond. "We're best friends," Kellan told *Seventeen*. "When we were younger, he'd get his phone confiscated and be like, 'Kellan, bring me yours!' And it'd be like midnight and I'm sliding it down the hallway to him. He took advantage of me but the roles switched when I got older. He was a senior when I was a freshman. And he was like, 'Kellan, you're cool now. Let's hang out.' He brought me to the parties and I was like the cool young Lutz."

Kellan was very athletic from an early age, and played all sorts of sports. He particularly loved anything involving the outdoors, which makes sense since Dickinson is known for its beautiful scenery. Kellan hunted, hiked, camped, and skied every chance he got. As he got older, he expanded his interests to include whitewater rafting, skydiving, parasailing, snowboarding, and motorcross racing. He also had one other very unusual hobby—signing his name! "I like signatures," Kellan told about.com. "I remember growing up just having fun doing it for no reason. I'd always want to sign a check when

I was younger so I was like practicing . . ." That practice has certainly served him well now that he's always being asked for his autograph!

Kellan also discovered a taste for scary movies early on. "My father didn't really get that kids shouldn't watch PG-13 movies until they're 13, or R-rated movies until they're 17," he told amctv.com. "He'd rent horror movies and watch them with us. He took me to see *Scream* when I was about 8—and I loved it! My mother, on the other hand . . . when I did [the 2008 movie] *Prom Night*, she swore if I ever did something scarier than that, she wouldn't go see it. And that was just a PG-13 thriller." Clearly, Kellan's love of the supernatural was early training for his role in the *Twilight* movies, even if he didn't know it yet!

When he was fourteen, Kellan's mom remarried, and the family settled in Arizona. His new stepdad had two sons of his own, so suddenly Kellan found himself the youngest of four brothers. It was a major change for him, and he decided to face it head-on, getting involved in drama and sports and earning attention despite being in a new city, a new state, and a new family. It was a whole different world for him, and he decided he wanted to explore every part of it. His curiosity and eagerness to explore and learn about everything is something that still shapes Kellan today.

Family wasn't the only new thing in Kellan's life, however. As he related to newfaces.com, "A friend of mine was always modeling for Dillard. Being gone from school sounded good to me so I talked to one of my best friends about looking for an agency. He told me about the Ford Agency—a top agency that casts on New Faces—I signed with them and I was on my way." Kellan was already well on his way to his eventual height of six foot one, and his height, rugged good looks, impressive physique, and blond curls got him plenty of attention—and plenty of modeling jobs! He did several ads for Levi's Jeans, and quite a few for the popular clothing chain Abercrombie & Fitch, culminating in the cover of their 2004 catalog.

During high school, Kellan also had an amazing opportunity that introduced him to what would become another lifelong pleasure. His school had a semester abroad program, and Kellan took advantage of it, spending a semester studying and traveling in the Dominican Republic. He became fluent in Spanish as a result, and had a wonderful time, but he also saw how many people outside America struggled just to survive, which gave him a greater appreciation of life and family and good fortune. And the thing he fell in love with? Travel. "I love traveling," he told about.com. "I love it, love it, love it, and that's one of the pros about being an actor. We get to shoot in so many different locations, especially movies. I've been to a lot of places in the world and there's so many more that I'd love to do, and that's what's kind of fun about picking projects. A lot of it goes in to, 'Where are we going to shoot?'"

Kellan graduated high school in 2003. Then it was a question of what to do next. His mother, stepfather, and his three new younger brothers and younger sister were all in Arizona, but Kellan had his sights set somewhere else. His father had moved out to California after the divorce, and that became a major factor in Kellan's decision of where to go after graduation. "I really wanted to get close to him because I never really had much of a relationship with him," Kellan told *MediaBlvd* magazine. "I'd see him once or twice a year." Of course, the fact that Kellan loved the beach may have also played a part in his decision to move toward the surf and sand!

Kellan had decided to pursue a degree in chemical engineering, and he got a scholarship to Orange County's Chapman University, so he packed his bags and headed out to California. He was off to college! He'd also toyed with the idea of joining the Navy and applying to become a Navy SEAL, but chose to pursue college and a more traditional job instead. Little did he know that he was about to discover a whole other career out there, one that would grab hold of him and refuse to let go!

# CHAPTER 4

# One from Across the Pond

Robert Thomas Pattinson was born on May 13, 1986, in Barnes, a suburb of London. His father, Robert, was a car dealer who imported vintage cars from America. His mother, Clare, worked for a modeling agency when Rob was growing up, which may have been a reason for his decision to pursue modeling later in his life. Robert grew up in a wealthy neighborhood near the Thames River, close to two significant landmarks that no doubt helped shape his interest in music and theater. The recording studio Olympic Studios has hosted some of the world's biggest rock stars, from the Beatles to Madonna to Coldplay, while the Old Sorting Office Arts Centre is well-known in both art and theater. In fact, Robert performed in several of the Old Sorting Office's stage productions during his teens. Talk about starting close to home!

Robert's first love wasn't acting, though. It was music. "I have been playing the piano for my entire life—since I was three or four," he told *Movie Magic* magazine. "And the guitar—I used to play classical guitar from when I was about five to 12 years of age." He set music aside for a while when he reached his teens (and he later revealed to the BBC that he was "really into rap" all through junior high, following artists like Eminem and Jay Kay from the group Jamiroquai), but it was always there in the back of his mind, and Robert would return to his music again a few years later.

Robert started his education at the Tower House School, an all-boys school that was known for its high standards. Music, art, and drama are part of the school curriculum, and Robert got his first taste of acting there at age six—not counting the times his sisters "used to dress [him] up as a girl and introduce [him] as 'Claudia'!" as he told bbc.com. Rob's early roles included the King of Hearts in a teacher-written play called *Spell for a Rhyme* and the character Robert in a stage production of William Golding's *Lord of the Flies*.

"He wasn't a particularly academic child but he always loved drama," school secretary Caroline Booth later told the *Evening Standard*. "I wouldn't say he was a star but he was very keen on our drama club. We're all so pleased that he's found something he really shines at."

Robert's family was happy to see him doing something creative. "My dad said to me the other day: 'I really am an artistic person,'" Robert revealed to virginmedia.com. "I was shocked as I never saw him as creative. I think me and my sisters are living out that side of him as my sister is another creative person, she's a songwriter." Robert's older sister Elizabeth, better known as Lizzy, is a singer and a songwriter. She was discovered by EMI, one of the biggest British record labels, when she was just seventeen, and has written for and sung with a number of successful bands, including the trio Aurora UK (along with keyboardist Simon Greenaway and guitarist Sacha Collisson), which had two top 20 hits, "Dreaming" and "The Day it Rained Forever," by the time she was eighteen. His oldest sister, Victoria, applies the Pattinson creativity to her work in advertising. Clearly Robert isn't the only talent in the family!

Unfortunately, Robert didn't shine at his schoolwork the same way he lit up the stage. "They were always pretty bad," he told the BBC about his report cards. "I never ever did my homework. I always turned up for lessons, as I liked my teachers, but my report said I didn't try very hard."

But nice, supportive teachers weren't enough to keep Robert interested and out of trouble, unfortunately. He got expelled from school when he was twelve! He's never revealed the reasons for his expulsion, but considering he switched to a coed school after that, and he told *Seventeen* that he got his first kiss at the same age, we don't think he minded much! "Twelve was a turning point," Robert admitted to bbc.com, "as I moved to a mixed school [a school with boys and girls] and then I became cool and discovered hair gel."

Rob's new school, the Harrodian School, was a different environment for him, and not just because both girls and boys attended. The faculty there encouraged their students to develop to their full potential in every area, and that included being as creative as possible. Robert told bbc.com his favorite teacher at Harrodian was: "Probably my English teacher because she got me into writing instead of just answering the question. I used to hand in homework with 20 pages of nonsense and she'd still mark it. She was a really amazing teacher."

As if school wasn't enough to keep him busy, Robert got a job! "I started doing a paper round when I was about 10," he said. "I started earning £10 [around twenty American dollars] a week and then I was obsessed with earning money until I was about 15." School and the paper route kept him busy, but after a while Robert accidentally stumbled upon something that would change his life forever. "My dad and I were at a restaurant and noticed this group of pretty girls nearby," he told virginmedia.com, "and for some reason decided to ask where they had just been. They mentioned the local acting school and since then [my father] had nagged me about attending. At one point he said he would pay me which is pretty strange—I don't know what his intentions were, but I went." And it's a good thing he did! Robert had always excelled on the stage, and now he finally had a chance to develop his love of acting. Off Robert went to become a professional actor—little did he know he would soon be a star!

# CHAPTER 5
# And Lautner Is Last

When Dan and Deborah Lautner, a young couple living in Grand Rapids, Michigan, had their first child, they knew right away that he was going to be very special. It was a cold winter day on February 11, 1992, when the Lautners welcomed Taylor Daniel into the world. He was absolutely adorable with his big, brown eyes and cap of dark hair, and it was easy to see he would be a charmer. After all, everyone at the hospital thought he was as cute as a button!

The family took baby Taylor home with them a few days later to their quaint little house on Rosewood Avenue in Grand Rapids. Dan worked as a commercial pilot, so he wasn't home to play with his son as often as he would have liked. But Deb worked for Herman Miller, an office furniture design firm nearby, so she got to spend plenty of time at home with her baby boy. And Taylor had lots of extended family close by, too. Dan's family lived in Traverse City, Michigan, and Deb's was in Manistee, Michigan. While his mom and dad were working, Taylor went to day care. He was very popular with the other kids there, but he did have one bad habit. "I was a biter at day care," Taylor told the *Grand Rapids Press*. "I don't remember it, but my parents tell me I'd bite other kids." Bet Taylor didn't know at the time that biting would play a big part in his future as an actor! Luckily, Taylor got over his biting phase fairly quickly, and he continued to be popular as he started elementary school.

Taylor was a very energetic and athletic little boy. He was obsessed with playing football, basketball, and wrestling, and he wanted to be a professional athlete when he grew up. He loved watching sports with his dad on TV and tossing the ball around. Taylor probably gave his mom quite a few scares running around the house and wrestling and playing with his friends. But the whole family got a *real* scare when Taylor was only four years old. Dan was away for the night on a flight, and Taylor and his mom were staying with Taylor's aunt for the evening. It's a good thing that no one was at home because that night the Lautners' house caught on fire and burned down. "The police called and told us our house had burned down," Taylor explained to the *Grand Rapids Press*. "If my aunt hadn't invited us to sleep over . . . well, wow." Taylor has never forgotten how frightening that night was. The family lost many of their belongings in the fire, but they were just thankful that no one had been hurt.

The family moved to a new, larger house in nearby Hudsonville, Michigan, to be closer to several of Taylor's aunts and uncles. And it's a good thing they did, because a couple of years later the family got even bigger. When Taylor was six years old, his baby sister, Makena, was born. Taylor loved being a big brother. He has always had a big imagination, and Makena loved playing the games he made up. "My sister and I would always be spies when I was younger. We'd be in the house, and I'd hide something, and I'd act like we were secret agents and spies. And I'd tell her that it was really happening, and she still believes me to this day," Taylor told radiofree.com. It's no surprise that Makena believed Taylor without question since she's always really looked up to her big brother. The two of them are still close, and Makena is always there to make sure Taylor doesn't get too full of himself now that he's a famous actor!

Around the time Makena was born, Taylor began to take sports more seriously. Taylor wanted to learn more about lots of different sports, but he was especially eager to take karate classes. So, after much begging on Taylor's part, his parents enrolled him in lessons at Fabiano's Karate & Fitness Center in Holland, Michigan. "A friend through my mom's work had his sons in karate and my parents took me to check out the class. I liked it and began karate when I was six. I really liked class because of all the games we got to play, like swords and spears, sensei says, etc. I didn't really care too much for the push-ups and all the hard work. I really started because of the fun games," Taylor told karateangels.com. Taylor caught on quickly in martial arts, and he was soon one of the best students in his classes. He loved just about everything about doing karate, "except for the part about being barefoot," Taylor explained to the *Grand Rapids Press*. "I don't like being barefoot. I don't even wear sandals."

Luckily Taylor didn't have to be barefoot when he was playing other sports like football, basketball, baseball, and horseback riding, and he was good at every sport he tried. But his absolute favorites were karate and football. He started playing on a football team when he was nine. "I love sports," Taylor told the *Grand Rapids Press*. "If there's an excuse to play football, I'm there." He excelled at both, but it was his standout performance in martial arts that really got Taylor noticed.

Taylor was a natural at karate. He loved his classes and he worked very hard outside of class to improve his skills. He advanced quickly and, within a year, he was winning all of the local competitions for his age level. "A lot of boys that age are bouncing off the walls, but Taylor was always deliberate, focused," Tom Fabiano, the owner of Fabiano's Karate and Taylor's childhood karate instructor, told the *Grand Rapids Press*. "He wasn't a typical kid. He always worked extra hard." In fact, when

Taylor was seven years old, Tom thought he was ready to begin competing against other students on a national level. So in 1999, Taylor attended his first national competition. He was so good that he brought home three first-place trophies! But, even more importantly, Taylor met a teacher who would help him take his martial arts skills to the next level—seven-time World Forms and Weapons Champion Mike Chat.

Mike Chat is an actor and martial artist who appeared as the Blue Lightspeed Ranger, Chad Lee, on the popular children's television show, *Power Rangers Lightspeed Rescue: The Queens Wrath*. Mike has won multiple local, national, and world karate competitions, and he was inducted into the World Martial Arts Hall of Fame in 1992. In addition to martial arts, Mike has also mastered tae kwon do, kickboxing, yoga, ballet, and acrobatics. Over time, he combined all of those things with karate to create a new form of martial arts that he called XMA, extreme martial arts. XMA is heavily influenced by the martial arts depicted on television, in video games, and in films like *Kill Bill: Vol. 1* and *2* and

*Crouching Tiger, Hidden Dragon.* Mike's new form of martial arts was entertaining and fun to watch, and it quickly became popular with many karate students, including Taylor! ". . . my favorite martial artist is Mike Chat. He's helped me so much," Taylor told karateangels.com. Mike has been so successful in martial arts because he flawlessly combines his physical skills and expertise with showmanship and charisma, and he's very well-known in the martial arts community.

Taylor had been a fan of Mike's long before he ever met him, so Taylor must have been pretty thrilled when Mike noticed him! "So I started [karate] and it was a lot of fun and I went to my first national tournament in Louisville, KY and then I met a karate instructor, Mike Chat, the Blue Power Ranger. He taught me this extreme martial arts stuff and I started liking that a lot more, so I kept doing it and I've been doing it for about six years," Taylor told kidzworld.com.

Mike invited Taylor to attend his XMA Camp at UCLA that summer. Taylor had only ever trained in traditional martial arts, so almost everything he learned at Mike's camp was new to him. He learned how to do flips, complicated jumps, and impressive kicks. "I fell in love," Taylor told the *Grand Rapids Press*. "By the end of the camp, I was doing aerial cartwheels with no hands." Mike was even more impressed with Taylor by the end of camp than he had been before. Taylor was perfect for XMA—he was a fast learner, physically skilled, and a great showman. Mike offered to train Taylor. The only problem was that Taylor and his family lived in Michigan and Mike was constantly on the road. But Taylor wasn't going to let a little thing like distance keep him from training with one of the best karate instructors around! So Mike and Taylor set up a training schedule, and Taylor would fly to Los Angeles to work with Mike as often as he could. "I try to get with my instructor, Mike Chat, as much as possible. He gives me homework assignments to work on at home. Then I go out with my Mom and Dad's help in trying to achieve my homework from Mike," Taylor explained to karateangels.com. Taylor worked very hard to improve his skills following Mike's training program.

For the next year, Taylor trained with Mike in extreme martial arts, while still competing on the North American Sport Karate Association circuit. And during that time, Taylor earned his black belt. Every karate student starts out with a white belt and then works to learn new skills. With each new set of skills a student masters, he gets a new colored belt to commemorate his rank. The black belt is the highest, most advanced rank. It was a very big accomplishment for Taylor to get his black belt before he was nine years old.

A lot of kids would have had a difficult time juggling traditional karate, XMA training, karate competitions, and other sports, friends, and schoolwork. But Taylor isn't most kids! With his parents' help, Taylor figured out a schedule that worked for him and he stuck to it, even if it meant taking an overnight flight back from Los Angeles so he wouldn't miss important tests. "I get mostly As with an occasional A- here and there. The key is an open communication with my teacher. My parents and me are in close communication with my teachers to make sure I'm not missing anything and understanding assignments. This doesn't mean it's not been difficult, because it has. I think once the school understands that my education is important to me, and then they are more understanding. The last week has been really tough. I've had to stay up till 10:30 or 11:00 PM each night to make sure all my homework is done," Taylor told karateangels.com.

When Taylor was eight, he was invited to compete for the USA at the World Karate Association Championships in the 12 and under age division. The best martial artists in the world come together to compete at the World Karate Association Championships, so it's a very big honor to even compete there. It's an even bigger honor to win—and Taylor won big. Taylor won three gold medals and became the Junior World Forms and Weapons Champion. Taylor was the best martial artist under the age of twelve in the entire world! That's a pretty big accomplishment for an eight-year-old. But Taylor wasn't done yet. That same year, Mike invited Taylor to join Team Chat International, his elite XMA competition squad. That was exactly what Taylor had been working toward since he met Mike, so he was probably very excited!

Taylor worked harder than ever to perfect his skills. When he was nine years old, he won the Warrior Trophy Cup for the 17 and under age group at a World Karate Association tournament in Chicago, Illinois. Taylor was thrilled with his accomplishments, but he was also a little burned out from karate. He had been focusing almost all of his time and attention on karate for over three years. So Taylor decided to take a year off from competitions, although he continued to train. He also took that time to focus on other sports, like baseball and football. "My training schedule changes depending on the time of year. I try to train 3-4 times a week, but during football season, 4 times per week could be a little tough to fit in," Taylor told karateangels.com. Training as hard as he did, Taylor became a truly well-rounded athlete. He was just as good on the baseball and football fields as he was at martial arts, much to the amazement of his family and coaches. It's not very often that an athlete as skilled as Taylor comes along, and everyone was very impressed.

Taylor had a great time playing football,

baseball, and spending more time with his friends, but it wasn't long before Taylor missed karate too much to stay away. In early 2003, Taylor rejoined the competition circuit. Also, at the beginning of the 2003 karate season, Mike invited Taylor to join his new XMA Performance Team, which was sponsored by Century Fitness, Inc. The team performed their coolest and most advanced tricks at competitions, sporting goods stores, and professional basketball games. Taylor loved being in the spotlight and performing for fans. "From karate, I had the confidence and drive to push myself," Taylor told the *Grand Rapids Press*. He worked harder than he ever had before, and that year he was ranked number 1 in the World at the North American Sport Karate Association's Black Belt Open Forms, Musical Weapons, Traditional Weapons, and Traditional Forms. Then, in July 2003, Taylor won the World Junior Weapons Championship.

Taylor had proven that he had the dedication, work ethic, and talent to be the best in the world in both XMA and traditional karate for his age. And that's no small feat considering that martial arts are practiced in almost every single country in the world. Sadly, when Taylor's acting career really took off, he had to give up competing. But he still trains and he'll be ready to use those martial arts skills in his future acting!

# CHAPTER 6
# Getting the 411

Jackson Rathbone joined his musician friend Alex Boyd out in Los Angeles, and Alex soon introduced Jackson to his own manager, Pat Cutler of Cutler Management. Pat was impressed with Jackson's acting ability and obvious charisma, and signed him immediately. She wanted him to study film acting, since he had no prior experience there, and sent him to learn from Jeremiah Comey, a former Fulbright scholar who had been teaching film acting in Hollywood for over twenty-five years. She also started sending Jackson out on television and film auditions. One of his first was with the Disney Channel, for a new show called *Disney 411*, which was essentially an interview and news segment for the network. And Jackson won the part!

He was excited, both because it gave him his first television credit and because it meant he got to interview Disney stars like Hilary Duff and Raven-Symoné. Jackson's skills attracted interest from Paradigm talent agent Andrew Ruf, and he soon signed Jackson as well. Now Jackson had a team behind him, with Andrew, Pat, and, of course, his buddy Alex providing support. The summer passed all too soon, and Jackson had a tough decision to make. Things were just starting to take off for him in L.A., but he was expected at the Royal Scottish Academy for school in the fall. Should he stay or should he go? Should he return to the stage, or stick with film?

It was a difficult choice, but in the end, Jackson decided to remain in Los Angeles for the time being. As he told examiner.com, "I moved to L.A. for the summer to work on music as a songwriter . . . but my manager, Cutler Management, started a lot of work for me when I had no resume, so . . . I stayed to become an actor . . . thanks to fan support!" He makes it sound so simple, and in a way it was, as all the pieces just fell into place for him. Jackson and Alex got a place together, and since Alex was focused on his music career, the pair got to work setting up a recording studio in their new living room. Meanwhile, Andrew sent Jackson out on a series of auditions for everything from films to commercials.

Jackson landed several commercials, and then got a bit part in a movie called *River's End* (also known as *Molding Clay*). Interestingly enough, the movie was being shot in Texas, not far from Jackson's hometown! *Molding Clay* was directed by William Katt, best known for his television show *The Greatest American Hero*, which ran from 1981 to 1983 and starred Katt as a high-school teacher turned bumbling superhero. That series also starred Barry Corbin (a veteran character actor who was on *Northern Exposure* for its full five-year run and has played Coach Whitey Durham on *One Tree Hill* for the past six years) as Sheriff Buster Watkins, a Texas sheriff who tries to straighten out his teenage grandson.

The movie released in 2007, after several of Jackson's other projects had already aired. It was valuable experience for Jackson nonetheless, and only convinced him that he'd made the right choice in opting for Hollywood over the theater.

Next, Jackson appeared on an episode of the TV show *Close to Home*. The legal drama revolves around Jennifer Finnigan as Annabeth Chase, a young prosecutor who returns to work after having her first child and tries cases from her own neighborhood, now more determined than ever to protect her community and her family. The show ran on CBS from 2005 to 2007. The episode, "Romeo and Juliet Murders," involved two teenagers who are found with narcotics when their party is busted. The teens say their parents are on vacation in Europe, but no one can seem to find them—until two bodies are discovered in the woods, and murder charges are added to the teens' drug charges. Jackson's character Scott Fields was one of the teens' friends. It was a great experience for Jackson, and soon after that he won a role in an independent thriller called *Pray for Morning* from writer/director Cartney Wearn. The movie revolves around a group of highschool students who decide to sneak into the abandoned and supposedly haunted Royal Crescent Hotel for a night of fun and wind up awakening an old evil that begins hunting them in turn. The film also starred Udo Kier (best known for his many vampire movies, from Andy Warhol's *Blood for Dracula* to the Wesley Snipes' movie *Blade*), Jonathon Trent, *90210* actress Jessica Stroup, Dennis Flanagan, Ashlee Turner, Brandon Novitsky, Kip Martin, Rachel Veltri, Robert F. Lyons, and Peter Pasco. One cast member in particular taught Jackson a great deal. In an exclusive interview with the fansite jackson-rathbone.com, Jackson revealed, "On my very first film, I got to work with Udo Kier, a celebrated German actor. He revealed little insights to me on the subtleties of film acting. One of the most important; to learn from everyone around you. Being on set is like being paid to go to film school."

Despite being busy with acting, Jackson kept up with his music as well. He and Alex wrote songs together on the side, and performed as a band at occasional gigs at small clubs and local bars. The two friends also formed Prolifik Productions, a small music studio that operated from their new home recording studio. That meant keeping the living room neat, though, which was difficult for Jackson, who's a self-avowed slob. "I keep a very messy room," he told *Portrait* magazine. "I am a very messy person! The only neat room is the living room because that's what visitors see and where we hang out! Also there's a small recording studio in the living room so it needs to be clean. The rest of the house suffers though . . . even my car is messy!"

Jackson was getting more and more work, both in television and in film. In 2006, he appeared on two episodes of the hit FOX show *The O.C.* as a character named Justin—the two episodes, "The Heavy Lifting" and "The Sister Act" involved Marissa's younger sister Kaitlin, and Jackson played her boyfriend who follows her there from her Montecito boarding school. Then he played the role of Travis in the Hallmark made-for-TV movie *The Valley of Light* (starring Chris Klein as a homeless World War II veteran who settles in a small North Carolina town and develops relationships with a lonely war widow and a mute boy who was abandoned by his father) and two episodes of the family comedy *The War at Home* (playing Dylan in "Kenny Doesn't Live Here Anymore" and "No Weddings and a Funeral"). After that, Jackson won the part of Robbie the Hippie in *Big Stan*, which starred comedy actor and former *Saturday Night Live* cast member Rob Schneider as Big Stan, a crooked real-estate agent who gets caught and sentenced to prison but, with the help of a mysterious guru (played by the late *Kung Fu* legend David Carradine), becomes a martial arts master and brings peace to the prison yard. The parts varied wildly, but Jackson loved that. He'd always enjoyed taking on different roles, and these gave him a chance to show the true breadth of his acting ability. But the best was still to come!

# CHAPTER 7
# Becoming a Model Citizen

Kellan arrived in California in 2003 and enrolled at Chapman, but the upcoming fall classes weren't the only thing on his mind. As he told newfaces.com, "In the summer before my first year at Chapman University (where I was going for chemical engineering) I booked a national Levi's campaign and Abercrombie and Fitch campaign and I had a lot of fun doing that. The more work I did, of course, the more people I met. I met a lot of agents in the process and found that there were many acting opportunities out there for me and with their help it really gave me a chance to try another love of mine." There were a lot more opportunities out in California than there had been in Arizona, and Kellan's successes back home intrigued people in Hollywood enough to get him noticed.

But that was modeling. Kellan noticed something

else, and that was, as he told *MediaBlvd* magazine, that "everyone and their mother was an actor." Kellan started to receive offers for acting jobs while he was a model, but at that point, he didn't have any real training for it. But he had always enjoyed acting, so he decided to take some classes. "I saw the passion in everyone's eyes," he continued, "and just really fell for it and loved it and wanted it. I saw how much fun people were having, enjoying life. In a way, it keeps you young. So, I started doing that, and I found myself a manager."

Classes had started by then, and Kellan managed to juggle his acting classes and his first few auditions with his schoolwork. Until the end of the semester, that is. "I remember my first call-back was on finals day of my first semester at Chapman," he recounted to *MediaBlvd* magazine. "I had to decide what to do. I thought call-backs meant that it would be down to me and one other guy, and I would get the role. I couldn't do finals because I thought that would start my career. And, wow, was I wrong! I did the call-back and didn't go further at all. I realized there were three other call-backs after that, and then a screen test, and then you get it. I was really bummed, and I failed all those classes." Kellan was disappointed, of course, but the experience taught him something important, too. He was sorry he hadn't gotten the role, and sorry he'd done poorly in his classes as a result—but he knew he'd make the same decision again in a heartbeat. As much as he enjoyed chemistry and engineering, he loved acting more than the two combined. And that meant he had to pursue his acting full-time if he really wanted things to work out. "I can always do school later," he told hollywoodpoker.com, "but I will always get older and might as well do what I enjoy in life, whatever it may be." Fortunately, it doesn't look like that's ever going to be an issue for him!

At the time, however, Kellan had no guarantee that he'd be able to make a living at acting. He knew he wanted to go for it anyway, but he still had to let his family know his decision. As he said to *MediaBlvd* magazine, "The hardest decision in my life was to tell my mother, 'Hey, mom, I want to pursue this other thing.' And, she had no idea what acting really was. Coming from the Midwest, acting was unheard of. We had four or five channels back then, and you never really thought that real people were on these shows. I never even knew acting was a profession and an occupation. So, I put school on hold. You can always go back to school. I was 18, at the time, and I just wanted to do it." Clearly Kellan has never been one to do things halfway!

His parents weren't too happy about his decision, of course. But it was Kellan's life, and they couldn't stop him from following his dreams.

The first thing Kellan did was find himself an agent. He studied acting full-time, went to every audition he could, and worked at honing his skills every second of every day. He met a lot of great people—including a fellow actor around his age named Jackson Rathbone, who Kellan became friends with after they ran into each other at several different meetings and auditions. The boys didn't know at the time that their paths would cross again, in a big way! Kellan worked really hard on his acting, and eventually all his hard work paid off and he started landing roles.

His first role was on the long-running soap

opera *The Bold and the Beautiful,* which is all about beautiful people behaving badly! Kellan must have fit right in! He played Rob on episode 1.4409 (the show doesn't use episode titles), which aired on October 19, 2004. Kellan was only nineteen years old at the time.

Next, he guest starred as Alex Hopper on an episode of the police-forensics procedural *CSI: New York.* The episode, "Tri-Borough," begins with a young man known only as Slick who is found dead across a subway rail. It looks like he died from electrocution, but an autopsy reveals otherwise. Meanwhile, an art gallery owner named Leo Whitefield is found shot dead near his gallery, and a construction worker is discovered with a fatal head injury. Kellan's character, Alex, is friends with Randy Hontz, the young man the team had labeled "Slick," and helps provide important information that leads to the capture of Randy's murderer. After that, Kellan played Critter on the episode "Hold My Hand" for the mortuary-centered TV series *Six Feet Under*—the episode focuses on George Sibley (played by veteran actor James Cromwell) dealing with the anniversary of his mother's suicide while the other members of his family deal with their own personal crises. Then it was on to the role of Fordie in two episodes of the WB drama *Summerland*, about three kids from Kansas who move to California to live with their struggling clothing-designer aunt after their parents are killed in a car accident. *Summerland* was set near—and often on—the beach, so it was perfect for a surfer dude like Kellan!

Then, in 2005, Kellan got an even bigger break. Lisa Kudrow, known worldwide as the ditzy Phoebe from the long-running hit comedy *Friends*, was starring in a new sitcom on HBO. Called *The Comeback*, its plot hit pretty close to Kudrow's own life—she plays Valerie Cherish, a former sitcom star struggling to revive her flagging career. And Kellan won the part of Chris MacNess, an actor who plays the surfer Mooner on the show-within-a-show *Room and Bored* and is the love interest of that show's star Juna (played by Malin Ackerman, who wowed audiences as the Silk Spectre in the movie *Watchmen*). This was Kellan's first recurring role on a series, and he loved it! He had the opportunity to work with a great cast and crew, including Kudrow, Ackerman, Laura Silverman, Damian Young, Craig DeSilva, and others. And it was nice to have some stability, and to get to develop a role more than he might have for just a guest spot. *The Comeback* only wound up running for thirteen episodes, and Kellan was in eight of them.

After *The Comeback* ended in 2005, Kellan went back to films for a while. He played Frank in the high school gymnastics movie *Stick It* (starring Missy Peregrym and Jeff Bridges); Dwayne in the teen comedy *Accepted* (about how several friends, played by Justin Long, Jonah Hill, Adam Herschman, and Columbus Short, create a fake university to convince their parents they got into college); and Chad in the direct-to-video horror movie *Ghosts of Goldfield*, about a group of filmmakers who venture to the abandoned town of Goldfield hoping to capture footage of the ghost rumored to haunt the place.

Then Kellan returned to television to guest star on *CSI: Crime Scene Investigation*—he played Chris Mullins in the episode "Empty Eyes," in which six showgirls and roommates are murdered in their home. One of the girls dies in Sara Sidle (actress Jorja Fox)'s arms, but not before leaving a vital clue to the killer's identity. Kellan also showed up on *Heroes*, where he played Andy in the episode "Chapter Twenty 'Five Years Gone,'" which took viewers five years into the future to see how the world would turn out if the heroes failed to prevent the disaster that was rapidly approaching in their own present.

Somewhere along the way, Kellan's parents came around to his way of thinking. "And now, my mother is happy because I brought her to the *Stick It* premiere for Disney," Kellan was able to report to *MediaBlvd* magazine. "She looked so beautiful, and just had so much fun seeing what Hollywood and acting really is, and that it's not the negative occupation that she thought it was. Everything is great now."

If Kellan's mom was happy about his success then, she must be utterly thrilled at how well her little boy is doing now!

# CHAPTER 8
# No Small Vanity

After leaving high school at age fifteen, Robert decided to try his hand at acting professionally. He wound up joining the Barnes Theatre Company, a local performance group that produced two shows a year. And when we say "local," we mean it—the company was around the corner from the house where Robert grew up! The strange thing is, though Robert had acted in school, he didn't really consider himself an actor. But his father did! As Robert told *Scholastic News*, "I really wasn't part of the acting fraternity at my school, but I joined this [acting group] after my dad argued with me for ages. I think he had some sort of weird foresight about it." Good going, Mr. Pattinson!

Of course, you don't just walk into a theater company and land leading roles—not even if you're Robert Pattinson! "I wasn't nervous of performing," he told *Stagecoach* magazine, "but at sixteen, I thought it would be arrogant [to admit that]!" So he started out working backstage, helping to build sets and change furniture. It was good experience for him, but it didn't last long. "For some reason when I finished the backstage thing, I just decided that I should try to act," he told *Scholastic News*. "So I auditioned for *Guys and Dolls*."

*Guys and Dolls* is a classic Tony Award-winning musical about gamblers and the ladies they love. Robert was hoping for the lead role of card shark Nathan Detroit—the same role Frank Sinatra played in the movie version. Instead, he was cast as one of the Cuban dancers! But Robert knew that every role counted, so he gave the part his full attention. And that paid off handsomely. As he explained to *Stagecoach*, "They respected me for doing it and gave me the lead in Thornton Wilder's *Our Town*—and that got me an agent."

After playing George Gibbs in *Our Town*, Robert went on to star in *Anything Goes*, a 1930s musical that features music and lyrics by Cole Porter. He played Lord Evelyn Oakleigh, who loses one fiancée and wins another during the course of the show. It was a fun musical, and Robert enjoyed himself, but that was the case during all his time with the Barnes Theatre Company. "They used to do two shows a year and they are all great," he told *Scholastic News*. "So many people from there had become actors. The directors were actors themselves and were very talented. I owe everything to that little club."

Since the Barnes Theatre Company only put on two shows a year, Robert looked for other acting jobs as well. He found them at the Old Sorting Office Arts Centre, another neighborhood feature. There he played Malcolm in Shakespeare's famous tragedy *Macbeth*, and Alec in *Tess of the D'Urbervilles*, a play based on Thomas Hardy's classic Victorian novel about a young woman whose family forces her to marry someone to improve their own situation.

The stage was not large enough to contain all of Robert's talent, however, and so with the help of his agent he made the transition to the big screen. In 2004, he got a part in the made-for-TV German movie *Ring of the Nibelungs* (also known as *Dark Kingdom:*

*The Dragon King*), which was based on the same legends as Richard Wagner's famous Ring Cycle operas and J. R. R. Tolkien's *Lord of the Rings*. The story revolves around the relationships between a hero named Siegfried, the warrior queen Brunnhild, a king named Gunther, and his sister, the princess Kriemhild. Robert played Giselher, the king's son. The most exciting thing about the role for him was that it took him out of England for the first time—and way out! The movie was filmed in Cape Town, South Africa! "I was there for three months in an apartment at just 17," Robert told virginmedia.com, "so I came back really confident." *Ring of the Nibelungs* also gave Robert his first experience with special effects, which he told virginmedia.com was "probably one of the strangest things to go into if you have never done acting before." But that certainly gave him good practice for the two big roles he would ultimately win: Cedric Diggory and Edward Cullen!

Next, Robert played a small part in the Victorian period movie *Vanity Fair*, which starred Reese Witherspoon (of *Legally Blonde* fame), Gabriel Byrne,

Jonathan Rhys Meyers, Bob Hoskins, and Eileen Atkins. Like *Tess of the D'Urbervilles*, the movie was adapted from a classic Victorian novel, which in this case was *Vanity Fair* by William Makepeace Thackeray. Witherspoon plays Becky Sharp, a young woman whose parents were poor artists who died and left her with nothing but her good looks, her sharp eye, her quick wit, a good deal of courage, and a fluent command of the French language. Using all of those to best effect, Becky proceeds to advance through the ranks of society, going from a poor orphaned girl to a wealthy and influential woman. Robert played Becky's grown son, Rawdy Crawley (the movie covers a span of twenty years). Unfortunately, Rob's scenes were cut from the theatrical release, but some of them can be seen as extras on the DVD. One cool aspect of that role was that Robert's best friend, Tom Sturridge, also had a small part in *Vanity Fair*. The two had met through Tom's brothers, who had attended Harrodian with Robert, and they had been friends for years.

It was around this time that Robert returned to music as well. "I didn't play guitar for like years," he told *Movie Magic* magazine. "About four or five years ago, I got out the guitar again and just started playing blues and stuff. I am not very good at the guitar, but I am all right. I am in a band in London as well." Robert later left that band, Bad Girls—at least in part because the band's founder was his first girlfriend's new boyfriend! But now that he'd rediscovered his love of music, Robert never forgot it, and he continued to practice and write songs even when he wasn't performing them anywhere.

Robert did some modeling during this period as well, under his full name, Robert Thomas-Pattinson. "He was painfully shy and incredibly polite," a *Life & Style* photographer recounted later. "He was a bit nervous too because I had him in some pictures with a girl. The shoot was based on swimwear from the 1930s. He had his shirt off, some skin might have made him nervous. He was very new to modeling, but he pulled through and was fine. The shots were class, not trashy." Obviously Robert eventually got over that nervousness, and he went on to model for several other companies before his chiseled good looks earned him a steady spot modeling for British clothing label Hackett. According to its website, Hackett "is a classic British clothing and accessories brand which caters for the head to toe needs of men of all ages who wish to dress stylishly and to whom quality is more important than the vagaries of fashion." Robert certainly fit the description, and he represented Hackett's Autumn/Winter 2007 clothing line along with several other young models.

Robert only modeled for a few years, however. Why did he stop? Well, Robert has his own theory. "When I first started," he told the British magazine *Closer*, "I was quite tall and looked like a girl, so I got lots of jobs, because that androgynous look was cool. Then, I guess, I became too much of a guy, so I never got any more jobs. I had the most unsuccessful modeling career." Hardly unsuccessful, but it's probably good that he didn't get any more modeling work—he wouldn't have had time for it! His acting career was taking off, and his biggest role yet was about to present itself—a role that would bring him to the attention of not just Britain, but the United States as well.

# CHAPTER 9
# The Phantom of Success

Taylor had already proven himself a whiz at martial arts, but when he was seven, his coach, Mike Chat, suggested that he try acting as well. Mike had been a successful actor himself, so he knew how to spot talent. "[Mike] saw that I wasn't shy, that I was confident, that I talked a lot," Taylor told the *Grand Rapids Press*. Taylor was a great showman and he was certainly at ease in front of a crowd—plus he had martial arts skills that film directors would love to have for action movies! Since Taylor was already traveling to Los Angeles frequently for karate, it would be easy for him to audition for roles. He was really excited about the idea of acting, so he convinced his parents to let him give it a shot.

Taylor soon went to his first audition for a Burger King commercial. It was 1999. "The first audition that my karate instructor sent me out on was a Burger King commercial. It was kind of like a karate audition in that they were basically looking for martial arts stuff. And they were looking for someone older, but he wanted to send me anyway to get the experience. So, I met with the casting director, we talked, and she asked for some poses. It was funny though, because at the time, I didn't even know what a pose was! I was only seven. But I learned quickly and did some poses for them. And I really liked it. I thought it went well, but I didn't get it . . ." Taylor told the *Oregon Herald*. Taylor didn't get the part, but he was determined to keep trying. Mike helped Taylor get an agent. After that, whenever Taylor was in Los Angeles to train with Mike, he let his agent know. If there were any auditions going on then, Taylor would try out.

In 2001, Taylor nabbed his first real acting role in *Shadow Fury*, an action, science fiction flick with some serious martial arts fights. In the film, the good guys are battling an evil mad scientist and his army of superstrong human clones. Taylor played the younger version of the character Kismet. Kismet is a fighter clone made to battle the bad clones. Taylor wasn't in the film for very long, but he did have an amazing fight scene where he killed one of the bad guys. Taylor gave an incredible performance, especially considering how little acting experience he had. With *Shadow Fury* on his résumé, Taylor became in demand and was soon flying to Los Angeles for auditions a few times a month. "They'd call at 9 or 10 at night, which was 6 or 7 their time, and say, 'We've got an audition tomorrow—can you be here?' We'd leave really early in the morning and get there about noon," Taylor told the *Grand Rapids Press*. "I'd go to the audition in the afternoon, take the red-eye back to Grand Rapids, then go to school."

By the time Taylor was ten, he was flying back and forth to Los Angeles regularly. Between that and all of the traveling the Lautners were doing for karate tournaments and training, the family was overwhelmed. "We decided, 'This is insane,'" Taylor explained to the *Grand Rapids Press*. "We can't keep on doing this." So, in 2002, the whole family made a difficult choice. They decided to pack their bags and move to Los Angeles—but only for a month to try it out. "It was a big deal to leave,"

Taylor told the *Grand Rapids Press*. "All our family was [in Michigan]." Taylor missed home, of course, but instead of focusing on his homesickness, he put all of his energy into acting. He went to tons of auditions, but he didn't book any parts. By the end of the month, it seemed like the family might be heading back to Michigan and Taylor might be giving up acting for good. Luckily, "I got one callback," Taylor told the *Grand Rapids Press*. "That gave me the drive to keep going. It happened on our very last day there." That one callback convinced Taylor and his parents that it wasn't time to give up Taylor's dream yet. So they decided to extend their stay in Los Angeles for six months.

Taylor made sure that his agent sent him out for any parts for boys his age during that time. "There were more auditions. I heard no, no, no, no, so many times," Taylor told the *Grand Rapids Press*. But Taylor would not be deterred. Eventually, he booked a job performing one of the voices in a commercial for Nickelodeon's *The Rugrats Movie*. "I thought, 'This is what I've been waiting for,'" Taylor told the *Grand Rapids Press*. It was a small role, but it was just the encouragement that Taylor needed. He and his family decided to stay in L.A. for good. "It was a very, very hard decision. Our family and friends did not want us to go. But our choices were: We could stay in Michigan and I could give up acting. (I would have had to because it would have been crazy to continually fly out from Michigan to California each time there was an audition!) Or we could move to California and I could continue to act. I told my parents I didn't want to give up acting. And after weighing the good with bad, they agreed to move. Of course, we were all sad that our house was gone in Michigan. But it turned out for the best because we're having a lot of fun in California now," Taylor told the *Oregon Herald*.

Moving away from his hometown was worth the sacrifice for Taylor. Once he and his family settled in to their new home, he booked job after job. In 2003, Taylor guest starred as a bully named Aaron on Fox's *The Bernie Mac Show* in the "Rope-a-Dope" episode. *The Bernie Mac Show* starred stand-up comedian Bernie Mac. On the show, Bernie has taken in his sister's children and a lot of the comedy was based on Bernie's unique parenting skills. Taylor had a blast on the set working with such a well-known and established comedian. He still considers it one of his favorite roles ". . . because I got to be a bully and push this little kid around! That was fun because I'm normally not a bully because my parents wouldn't allow me to do that. I'm just not that person, but it was fun to experience something new," Taylor explained to kidzworld.com. Taylor may have played a bully, but he got along with the rest of the cast very well and it made him eager to do more television work.

In 2004, Taylor played a boy on the beach on the hit teen drama *Summerland* (the same series that Kellan also guest starred on!) in an episode titled "To Thine Self Be True." Taylor had a very small role, but he was honored to work alongside a television veteran like star Lori Loughlin and teen heartthrob Jesse McCartney. Taylor didn't know it then, but he was well on his way to being an even bigger star than either of them!

Next, Taylor played Tyrone on ABC's *My Wife and Kids* in the episode "Class Reunion." *My Wife and*

*Kids* was a hilarious show starring Damon Wayans as a husband and father who was always getting into trouble. Taylor played a tough guy on *My Wife and Kids* who was bullying one of the show's characters. Damon Wayans and his family have all been very successful, so Taylor was probably thrilled to have the chance to work with them.

Then Taylor appeared on *The Nick and Jessica Variety Hour* alongside pop stars Nick Lachey and Jessica Simpson. It was a funny show filled with skits, music, and jokes. Taylor appeared in some of the skits. He especially loved working with Jessica, and when asked who he would like to work with in the future, he was quick to give her name to kidzworld.com. "Jessica Simpson! Yeah, I'll work with her! I was on the *Nick and Jessica Variety Hour* show and that was lots of fun. I got to meet her, she was nice." Taylor impressed everyone he worked with on those television shows with his professionalism, talent, and good-natured attitude.

Taylor was having a lot of success guest starring on television, but in 2005 he discovered another way to flex his acting muscles—voice-over work!

Taylor had done some voice-over work for a few commercials and radio spots, but when he was thirteen years old he got the chance to provide the voices for several cartoons. In Taylor's first cartoon, he was the voice of "Youngblood" in Nickelodeon's *Danny Phantom*, a cartoon about a boy named Danny who can turn into a ghost whenever he wants. Danny must use his ghost powers to stop other ghosts from wreaking havoc on his town. Youngblood is a pirate ghost who appears in many episodes of the show. "My favorite [character to voice] so far was probably Youngblood on *Danny Phantom*. I've done three episodes so far and he's a lot of fun to voice. Probably because I'm a kid-bully-pirate. I'm an evil ghost and a pirate and get to say stuff like: 'ARRRGH!' " Taylor told the *Oregon Herald*. It was the first time that Taylor had appeared multiple times on one show and he liked the steady work and the chance to really get into his character and make him as funny as possible.

After *Danny Phantom*, Taylor signed on to do voice work on the Cartoon Network show *Duck Dodgers*. The show is about the classic cartoon character Daffy Duck and his adventures as a space-age superhero traveling the universe. It was a hilarious show, and Taylor was a fan even before he worked on it! A little bit later that same year, Taylor got the opportunity to become a part of another classic cartoon show when he signed on to work on *What's New, Scooby Doo?*, a cartoon based on the popular 1960s cartoon *Scooby Doo, Where Are You?*. Taylor provided the voice of Ned in the episode "A Terrifying Round with a Menacing Metallic Clown" and the voice of Dennis in "Camp Comeoniwannascareya." It was an especially exciting role for Taylor since two of the original *Scooby Doo* actors, Frank Welker and Casey Kasem, were working on the show. It must have been very cool to work alongside such cartoon greats!

The next year, 2006, Taylor continued his voice-over work with two special *Peanuts* cartoons, "Kick the Football, Charlie Brown" and "He's a Bully, Charlie Brown." The *Peanuts* characters, including Charlie Brown, Snoopy, Linus, Lucy, Peppermint Patty, and Sally, were created in the 1950s by the famed cartoonist Charles Schulz. It was first a comic strip in newspapers and then animated specials were created in the 1960s. Both the comic strips and animated cartoons have been a part of American culture ever since, and Taylor has always been a big fan. Taylor played Franklin in "Kick the Football, Charlie Brown" and a bully named Joe Aggit in "He's a Bully, Charlie Brown."

Taylor also did voice-over work for some lesser-known animated series. He provided the goofy voice of Silas on the short-lived series *Silas and Brittany*, which appeared on the Disney Channel. *Silas and Brittany* was a funny show about a pampered pooch and a silly cat that get stranded in the jungle together. Taylor also starred as Orley in the pilot of a show called *Which Way is Up?*, which never made it on the air. He was featured in a number of commercials and radio spots for products like Kellogg's Frosted Flakes, Sunkist, Superfresh, Petsmart, and Legoland. In addition to all of the voice-over work Taylor was doing, he also found time to guest star on *Love, Inc.*, a show on the now defunct UPN. *Love, Inc.* was about a group of friends running a dating service. Taylor played Oliver, a twelve-year-old boy trying to get the attention of his first crush, in the episode titled "Arrested Development." He was adorable on the show and the entire cast was totally charmed by him.

Taylor was making great headway in his acting career and booking work fairly steadily, but he wasn't content just to act. He continued to compete in martial arts, joined his school football team as a running back and middle linebacker, and played center field and second base as part of the Hart Baseball Program, a highly competitive baseball league in Los Angeles. Most kids would have had their hands full with just that, but not Taylor! He began taking dance lessons in 2003, and he caught on quickly. Soon, he was so good that he was able to join two performance dance groups, L.A. Hip Kids, a hip-hop dance crew, and Hot Shots, a jazz dance group. Performing with the dance groups helped Taylor stay in shape and he loved being in the spotlight—not to mention the fact that he just loves to dance! Not many teenage boys would admit to that, but Taylor is proud of his skills. He also took voice lessons and even recorded a few songs with some of his friends. Taylor has no plans to pursue a music or dance career, but he prides himself on being a triple threat, so he may sign on to star in a musical someday!

Taylor was well on his way to being a well-respected actor with continuous gigs, but he wanted more than that. Taylor wanted to be a *star*. He had made the move to Hollywood. He had left behind his family, friends, and home. And now he was working hard on his skills in dance, music, sports, and acting. All Taylor needed was a chance to audition for a film. He knew that once he got that chance, he would blow the director away.

# CHAPTER 10
# Maybe a Little Hurt

Jackson had been getting regular roles, and his parts were growing larger with almost every movie or series. His next role was on a TV series called *Beautiful People*. The show, which aired on ABC Family from August 8, 2005, to April 24, 2006, focused on a family that moved from New Mexico to New York City to get a fresh start. Daphne Zuniga (who played Jo Reynolds on the 1990s TV series *Melrose Place*) stars as Lynne Kerr, who decides to make the change after parting ways with her husband. She eventually gets a job in fashion and begins working for a prominent sportswear designer. Torrey De Vitto (who later appeared on *One Tree Hill* as a psychotic nanny) plays her older daughter Karen, an aspiring model, and Sarah Foret plays younger daughter Sophie, a talented photographer whose work wins her a scholarship to the exclusive

Brighton School. Jackson played Nicholas Fiske, the charming and very rich heir to Fiske Publications and captain of the JV lacrosse team at Brighton. Nicholas falls for Sophie the minute he sees her, and abandons his current girlfriend, Paisley Bishop, to pursue her, creating a rivalry between Paisley and Sophie. Jackson was in fourteen of the show's sixteen episodes, which gave him an opportunity to experience the stability and structure of series life. Unfortunately, *Beautiful People* was canceled due to low ratings, but Jackson still came away from the show with valuable experience and another impressive credit to his name.

After *Beautiful People* came *Senior Skip Day*, where he played a slacker named Snippy. The movie focused on Gary Lundy (from *Donnie Darko* and *The Notorious Betty Page*) as Adam Harris, who is head over heels in love with Cara (*The Bold and the Beautiful*'s Kayla Ewell). Unfortunately, she is the most popular girl in school. On the one day of the year that he could actually have a chance with her, senior "skip day," he screws it all up by accidentally slipping the location of the party to the school principal, Frankfurt Dickwalder (Larry Miller). In a desperate attempt to salvage the situation, Adam moves the party to his own house instead. Needless to say, hilarity ensues. Tara Reid, Lea Thompson, Norm MacDonald, and Clint Howard also star. The movie was released on May 6, 2008.

After that, Jackson was back on television, in the episode "Back to One" of *The Cleaner*. Benjamin Bratt from *Law & Order* plays the lead character, William Banks, a man who was once an addict himself but took control of his life and now uses his own experiences to help others overcome similar problems. In the episode, Jackson plays Joey, a young man who is determined to help his sister Lisa.

It was around this time that Jackson also reconnected with his fellow Lost Boys, his gang of friends from high school. As he explained to *MediaBlvd* magazine, "Once we all graduated, we all went to different areas. Ben Johnson went to New York and Ben Graupner went to Scotland. They both went to college, and I moved out to L.A. to do the acting thing. And then, finally, about a year ago, Ben Graupner moved out here to L.A., and then Ben Johnson came out. We started playing [music] together, and it just sounded so sweet. It was just so much fun." Everything was really clicking for Jackson—his closest friends were back in his life, *and* he was booking tons of acting jobs.

Jackson was really excited about his next role—a part in the gothic thriller *Hurt*. Set in Arizona, the movie follows the Coltrane family as they struggle with the untimely death of husband and father Robert Coltrane. Forced to give up their affluent lifestyle, Helen Coltrane and her teenage children, Conrad and Lenore, move in with Robert's reclusive brother Darryl, who has a battered home far out in the desert. The family is still learning to adjust to their new life when they gain a new addition, a pretty but troubled girl named Sarah, who Darryl has also agreed to take in. Then a series of strange and tragic accidents occurs, and the Coltranes go from sorrow to terror as they try to figure out what is happening, and how to stay alive. The movie starred Melora Walters (who played Claudia in *Magnolia* and was also in *Matchstick Men*, *Cold Mountain*, *Big Love*, and others), William Mapother (perhaps best known as the enigmatic Ethan Rom from the TV series *Lost*), Johanna Braddy (who appeared in episodes of *Cold Case* and *The Riches*), Sofia Vassilieva (Ariel Dubois on the Emmy Award-winning series *Medium*), and Ava Gaudet (a series regular on the TV comedy *Ugly Betty*). Jackson played the son, Conrad Coltrane. "He's an artist who is trying to hold his family together in the aftermath of his father's death," Jackson revealed to jackson-rathbone.org. "He tries to make light of things, but inside he's wounded." Considering Jackson's love of horror movies and his penchant for playing character parts, the role seems like a perfect fit for him! And given his own musical and theatrical endeavors, playing an artist shouldn't have been much of a stretch. Actually, Jackson does have some artistic aspirations of his own—as he told MTV, when his band 100 Monkeys releases their first two albums, "Both are gonna feature some new, original artwork by *this guy* [points to himself]."

*Hurt* was great fun to make, and it had a lot of chills, a lot of thrills—and a surprising amount of gore! At one point, the blood in *Hurt* got to Jackson, though—literally! "I got covered with sticky blood that congealed to my hairy legs," he explained to jackson-rathbone.com. "The costume designer Michele, bless her, helped me by trying to cut me free, but we eventually had to go by the band-aid method. Rii-iip." Ouch! Though finished, the movie has yet to be released, but thanks to their delay they can now bank on Jackson's new star power! Little did he know when he finished *Hurt* that his next role would be even more horrifying—but that he would be on the other side of that potential terror!

# CHAPTER 11

## Big in Beverly Hills

After guest starring on the hit television shows *CSI* and *Heroes*, Kellan switched over to movies again for a while, doing two in a row. The first was *Prom Night*, a slasher movie that focused on Brittany Snow (of *The Guiding Light*, *American Dreams*, and *Nip/Tuck*) as Donna Keppel, a high-school senior whose entire family was murdered three years before by a deranged teacher who had become obsessed with her. The teacher, Richard Fenton (played by Johnathon Schaech from *Models Inc.*, *Time of Your Life*, and *That Thing you Do!*), was sent to prison for life, but on the night of Donna's senior prom he escapes and comes after her, killing anyone who gets in his way. It's a race against time as Donna and her friends attempt to survive the horror on what should have been the best night of their young lives. Kellan played Rick Leland, one of Donna's friends and classmates. Did his character survive? You'll have to watch and see!

Next up was *Deep Winter*, an action-adventure flick about two friends who set out to ski a dangerous mountain peak in Alaska. Eric Lively, who was on *So Weird*, *A Minute with Stan Hooper*, *The L Word*, and *Modern Men* plays the lead, a maverick downhill racer named Tyler Crowe. Kellan plays his buddy and ski partner, renegade snowboarder Mark Rider. Michael Madsen, whose numerous film credits include *Thelma & Louise*, *Reservoir Dogs*, *Free Willy*, *The Getaway*, *Mulholland Falls*, and *Kill Bill Vol. 1* and *2*, plays their guide Dean, and Robert Carradine (best known for his role in the *Revenge of the Nerds* movies) plays Coach Dando, the boys' ski team instructor. This was the first time Kellan got major billing—the posters and the DVD cover list him as one of the movie's main stars! Plus, Kellan was probably psyched that his role included some time on the slopes—he's not afraid to profess his love for skiing!

Then it was time to return to television, only this time as a regular character on a short-run series. And on cable! Filming the series turned out to be a little bit more dangerous than Kellan expected, though, mostly because the show, while it is supposed to take place in the war-torn country of Iraq, was actually filmed in Mozambique. Mozambique was a dangerous enough place, and turned out to have its own set of problems that the cast had to deal with. As Kellan told about.com, "I did a mini-series. It's called *Generation Kill* for HBO . . . pretty much we had to shoot to mask Iraq, so we shot, like when we were in Mozambique we shot in Maputo which they just had a civil war 10 years ago so buildings are still crumbling and breaking down, and there's still security with AK-47s on every street corner. Like I got arrested so many times for the randomest things . . . I got pulled aside for wearing sunglasses during the day. Pulled aside for, I don't know, like wearing flip-flops I think. Like just anything and everything they'll do and all it takes is a couple of bucks and you're out of there . . . I don't think they realized what we were doing. I don't think they even cared about that. If anything, I think it was frowned upon that, you know, Americans are over here. 'What are they doing here?' It was kind of, it's different when you meet people who have no knowledge about what we do or why we're doing it."

The filming itself was difficult as well. "Tough, tough," Kellan told about.com. "A lot of sitting around. I played Jason Lilley and he was a Humvee driver so a lot of the scenes . . . There were massive scenes—we had tons of Humvees, real live equipment—and we're only driving 10 miles an hour. And then you drive down a road and then the roads are so small that you need to end up backing all the Humvees back, so that took hours. You're doing one scene. I remember we would shoot two pages a day and that's, I mean, 30 days to do one episode. It just blew my mind because I'm used to TV where it's maybe a week, maybe nine days. But here it's 30 days, and I didn't really think it would take so long. I thought I'd have time to come back to the US and see my family, maybe a week here or there. But I was there for seven months straight, six day weeks. It was tough but being with 39 other guys, it was a family. It was another life, but a family—like your frat years, in a way."

However, he told twilightcocoa.blogspot.com that *Generation Kill* had been his favorite role thus far. "I was able to play a marine," he explained, "and I have a brother who is in the marines he is currently in there for ten years. My stepfather he was in the air force. I just wanted to portray some war hero, on an epic journey and as a Marine we were able to shoot stuff and drive Hum-V's or blow up tanks. It's just a dream really to play a marine. It was really cool because I got to have my cake and eat it too because I really wasn't in any danger but yet could play the role of a marine." Still, "It was pretty crazy," Kellan admitted, "because I was shooting with 30 guys. We had 6 day work weeks, and we had a lot of down time and waiting around. So all we did was work out. And I gained a good 20 lbs. It was amazing and we just got yoked!"

After *Generation Kill*, Kellan got cast on another TV show, but this one was very different in tone, theme, and setting. "I landed a role on *90210*," he told twilightcocoa.blogspot.com, "they are bringing that show back and doing the remake and I'm really psyched about that because I have a lot of friends on it. I am really excited to do TV again and since the shoot is in LA, I can actually be around my dog and my friends. I have just been gone so much it's nice to be home." The show, which is more of a follow-up than a remake of the original series *Beverly Hills, 90210* that aired on Fox from 1990 to 2000, centers on the Wilson family as they move from Kansas to Beverly Hills to take care of Mr. Wilson's grandmother. The Wilson children, Annie and Dixon, enroll in West Beverly Hills High (the same school featured in the original series) and quickly develop both new friendships and new rivalries. Kellan plays star lacrosse player George Evans, who isn't very happy when Dixon Wilson not only makes the school team but also takes his spot on the starting lineup! "My character, George Evans, is the cocky [guy] of the school who just doesn't care," Kellan explained to *MediaBlvd* magazine. "He's from a rich family. If he got suspended, he'd pay his way out. He's supposed to be the lacrosse star, and then Dixon (Tristan Wilds) comes in and steals his thunder, so he really gets pissed. He never likes to be second place. I'm having a lot of fun playing him. I can't wait for his story to develop some more." Kellan likened George to two of the original series' main characters, telling MTV, "George is so the Luke Perry of the show. And maybe a little Brian Austin Green. I think they morphed the two of them. That's so where I'm taking George, just to let you know." Luke Perry's character Dylan McKay was the show's rebellious anti-hero, and Brian Austin Green's David Silver was a young whiz kid who battled with drug issues and had aspirations of music stardom. The first episode of the new version aired on the CW on September 2, 2008. On May 11, 2009, CW executives announced that they had renewed *90210* for a second season, and they hired Rebecca Rand Kirshner to head up both the second and the expected third seasons.

Kellan enjoyed working on the series, but his character wasn't crucial to most of the storylines. This proved to be a good thing, because it meant he could still pursue other projects during his downtime. Still, he told MTV that he hoped he would get more screen time as George in the second season, with "new drama in the new zip." Of course, his next project proved to be far too big to film between episodes and took him to a different zip entirely, far from sunny Beverly Hills, but it was well worth it!

# CHAPTER 12
# Harry Potter's Role Model

Robert had been enjoying his time onstage, and his first few small roles in film. But in 2003, he received a tremendous opportunity: an audition for *Harry Potter and the Goblet of Fire*.

The Harry Potter franchise began in 1998 with the book *Harry Potter and the Sorcerer's Stone* by J. K. Rowling, which detailed the life and adventures of Harry Potter, a young wizard whose parents had died at the hands of the evil Lord Voldemort. Harry had been raised by his "muggle" (meaning "nonmagical") aunt and uncle, and didn't even know about his heritage or his own abilities until his eleventh birthday, when he was whisked away to Hogwarts, the school of wizardry. There he made several close friends, learned about his family, and developed his magic, while Voldemort began once again to pursue his dreams of total conquest. The seventh and final book of the series, *Harry Potter and the Deathly Hallows*, was published in 2007. The series has sold more than 400 million copies worldwide and has been translated into over sixty languages. The last four books each set records as the fastest-selling books in publishing history!

In 2003, when Robert was seventeen, the long-awaited fifth book, *Harry Potter and the Order of the Phoenix*, had finally been published, and movies of the first two books, *Harry Potter and the Sorcerer's Stone* and *Harry Potter and the Chamber of Secrets*, had become smash hits. The third movie was in production, and the movie executives were already looking ahead to the fourth, *Harry Potter and the Goblet of Fire*. The same casting agent who suggested Robert for *Vanity Fair* suggested him for *Goblet of Fire*.

The day before Robert left for South Africa to start filming *Ring of the Nibelungs, Goblet's* casting agent introduced him to Mike Newell, the director of *Goblet of Fire*, and Robert auditioned for a role in the movie. "It was before anyone else had been seen for the other parts, so it was quite a cool position to be in. They did the rest of the casting for it afterwards," Robert explained to *Scholastic News*. He wasn't convinced he had done well, however, but kept his fingers crossed that he'd get good news.

Turns out, Rob must not have done badly at all, because he got a callback for *Goblet of Fire* the day after he returned from South Africa. He met with Mike Newell again, and after this second audition, Newell told Robert he was being cast as Hufflepuff Seeker, Head Boy, Triwizard Champion, and all-around nice guy Cedric Diggory. Robert was floored. "Since I started acting it's kind of been a bit mad," he later told virginmedia.com. "I never really did anything before and two years ago I started acting and I've kind of been in work ever since. Then *Harry Potter* came along and it's been a huge step and a massive event in my life." But little did he know it was just the first step of many to come!

So what did Robert think of Cedric? "I think he's a pretty cool character," Robert told bbc.com. "He's not really a complete cliché of the good kid in school. He's just quiet. He is actually just a genuinely good person, but he doesn't make a big deal about it or anything. He's just like, whatever. I can kind of relate to that. He's not an unattractive character at all and his story line is a nice story line to play."

In fact, Cedric is one of the nicest people in the entire Harry Potter series. "It's impossible to hate Cedric. He's competitive but he's also a nice guy," Robert explained to the *London Evening Standard*. Cedric is definitely the guy every girl wants to be with, and every guy wants to be. That's a lot to live up to! But Mike Newell was confident he'd made the right casting choice. "Cedric exemplifies all that you would expect the Hogwarts champion to be," he told the *London Evening Standard*. "Robert Pattinson was born to play the role; he's quintessentially English with chiselled public schoolboy good looks."

Interestingly enough, Robert himself doesn't think he's anything like Cedric. "Not at all," he told *Teen Vogue*. "I was never a leader, and the idea of my ever being made head boy would have been a complete joke. I wasn't involved in much at school, and I was never picked for any of the teams." But that just meant playing Cedric was more of a challenge, and Robert rose to the task. "Cedric is a really polite guy," he mentioned during an interview with a Japanese newspaper, "I wasn't really before. I became a lot more polite during the filming and I started holding open doors for people and things. And saying thank you for everything. People would say hello to me, and I would say thank you back."

This was by far the largest role Robert had yet landed, and with some of the most amazing actors he'd had a chance to work with. Did Robert find himself starstruck by some of the cast? He told bbc.com, "Yeah, I did. I'm a big fan of Michael Gambon [who plays the character of Dumbledore]. They were all really, really nice people and they treat it as a job. They don't really have big egos or anything about it. There was one guy—Warwick Davis—he's in *Willow*, and *Willow* is like my favorite film. I had one scene sitting next to him at the dragon task, and I had no idea what to say to him at all! He was the only person I asked for an autograph the whole way through it!"

Harry Potter fans the world over adored Cedric Diggory, so there was a lot of pressure on Robert to get the part right. Some of that was purely physical, too. As he told bbc.com, "In the book and also my first introduction of the script is like 'an absurdly handsome 17-year-old' and it kind of puts you off a little bit, when you're trying to act, and you're trying to get good angles to look good looking and stuff. It's really stupid; you'd think I'm really egotistical. But I think that's the most daunting part about it— it's much scarier than meeting Voldemort!"

One thing that helped Robert considerably was making a few new friends. In particular, he bonded with two of the other new cast members, Katie Leung (who played Cho Chang, Cedric's girlfriend and also Harry's crush) and Stanislav Ianevski (who played rival Triwizard competitor and quidditch star Viktor Krum). The three of them helped each other through the initial bout of nerves they all experienced from joining such a stellar cast that had already done three films together. Not that the other actors shut them out; in fact, Mike Newell took steps to make sure actors old and new felt comfortable together. "We had two weeks of acting classes," he explained at a press conference, "and the reason that we did this was that I was very anxious that the established characters would not dominate the newcomers, many of whom had never acted before. What we did was we played. We did physical exercises, we did improvisation exercises, and so on and so forth. And by the end of that, everybody was loose in one another's company." The result? "I didn't notice the transition to being accepted," Robert admitted to virginmedia.com, "but they are all really nice people. It seems like it should have been daunting but it wasn't."

Of course, Cedric wasn't needed in every scene—plus there was extra downtime because Daniel Radcliffe, who plays Harry Potter, was still in school and had to spend several hours every day working with his tutor on the set. So what did Robert do to pass the time? "I was just sitting by myself for ages," he recounted to iesb.net, "and at the time I wanted to be taken really seriously as an actor so I used to just sit around just drinking coffee all day and trying to look really intense."

When he was on-screen, Robert found a use for all that caffeinated energy! "I had to do a lot of fitness regimes and things in the beginning," he told *Film Review* magazine. "I thought that would be pretty cool, because it would make me take it seriously. It was run by one of the stunt team, who are the most absurdly fit guys in the world. I can't even do ten press ups. I did about three weeks of that, and in the end I think [the trainer] got so bored of trying to force me to do it that he wrote it all down so that I could do it at home." But Robert made sure to keep up with his exercises. He had to if he wanted to be able to play his role effectively. As he told virginmedia.com, "It's a very physical part. The stuff in the maze, which was done in the beginning, was all on huge action sets. The hedges were huge and hydraulically operated. I got hit by stuff, getting pulled around by ropes, and Dan [Radcliffe] and I were running around punching each other so it was kind of vicious!" He enjoyed it immensely, though. "The maze was really fun," he told bbc.com. "A lot of the stunts are very contrived, and someone's practiced them a hundred times and you have to get it perfect otherwise it's pointless doing it. You're not gonna be in the right shot or anything. But in the maze, a lot of it was on steadycam—which is just a guy running around with a camera . . . me and Dan were basically chasing each other around and punching each other, with these hedges squeezing us. And the camera would just follow you around, so you could basically do whatever you wanted. It was really fun. There were lots of cuts and bruises afterwards and it felt like you were doing a proper job!"

The maze wasn't the only physically demanding scene, either. "There was a lot of underwater stuff which I quite liked," Robert told virginmedia.com. "It got therapeutic after a while. I had never scuba dived before and the tank they taught us in was a little bathtub. The real thing was massive, like sixty feet deep and they expect you to just get in and act." He had a few hairy moments underwater, too, as he recounted to iesb.net. "There were a couple of times where you think you're swimming towards a guy with a breathing apparatus and then you find it's just some thing in the water. They film your stupid face just screaming underwater, and then everyone starts laughing and it's just like, ahh, great!" Still, working underwater had certain advantages. "You'd really concentrate on what you're supposed to be doing," he told bbc.com. "You can't talk to anyone so you stay completely in character. You can't see anything so all you can hear is your director through the water, saying like 'look scared.' It was pretty fun. It was really fun!"

Filming *Harry Potter* was an amazing experience for Robert. who had never experienced anything like it before. He told virginmedia.com, "The scale of Harry Potter is huge, people have been working on it for four or five years. There are 2000 people working on the set—not many films can afford that kind of 'epic-ness'."

Having that many people involved meant a lot of juggling schedules throughout. "There wasn't anything of any sort of structure," Robert admitted during a press conference before the movie's release. "There would be days where hardly anything would happen, where you'd stand around the whole time because it was such a long shoot. Everything was shooting for about eleven months or something in total, so there were days and weeks where you would do absolutely nothing." So what did he do? He got up early enough to be on the set at six-thirty, ate breakfast, had his hair and makeup done, got into costume, and was ready to work by nine, whether they needed him right away or not. "Some days were just ridiculously busy," he explained at the press conference, "while other days, especially when there is stunt work or something like that, [there was] a lot of time waiting around." But no one complained, least of all Robert. "It was a really long shoot so it was kinda tiring by the end," he told bbc.com, ". . . but all in all it was really fun, and there were a lot of amazing periods, which was really nice."

Little did Robert know the kind of attention he'd earn for playing Cedric—or the even bigger role it would lead him to sink his teeth into next!

# CHAPTER 13
# Shark in the Water

Taylor loved guest starring on television shows, but from the time he started acting, he'd always really wanted a shot at being a movie star. So when news got out that famed director Robert Rodriguez was filming a new children's movie and needed a couple of boys Taylor's age to star in it, Taylor jumped at the chance to audition.

Robert Rodriguez is the well-respected director of films like *Spy Kids, Spy Kids 2: Island of Lost Dreams, El Mariachi, Sin City, Desperado,* and *Once Upon a Time in Mexico.* He has a reputation in Hollywood for being a creative genius and actors love working with him. Robert takes big chances when it comes to his films, using cutting-edge special effects technology and choosing scripts that no one else would touch. For his newest film, Robert was developing an idea that his son had come up with about a boy named

Max who imagines two incredible superheroes when he is bored in school. The film was going to be called *The Adventures of Sharkboy and Lavagirl*, and Robert had decided to film in 3-D. Once he had the script ready, Robert and his family traveled all over the country looking for the perfect kids to play Max, Sharkboy, and Lavagirl.

Taylor went to the very first round of auditions in Los Angeles, but that meant he had to wait to hear back until all of the other auditions were over. "Unfortunately, L.A. was just the first spot that they stopped at before auditioning throughout the rest of the country," Taylor told the *Oregon Herald*. Taylor really wanted the role of Sharkboy. He knew he could use his martial arts skills in the movie to give Sharkboy an extra cool feel. Taylor definitely tried to work that into his initial audition, but he really got to show those moves off when he got a callback. "Well, my agent got me the audition to meet with the casting director. And I just did my scenes that my agent faxed to me. About two weeks later, we found out that Robert Rodriguez and his son, Racer (who came up with the idea for the film), wanted to meet with me at their hotel room in L.A. So, I went down and met with them and did my scenes for the casting director and Robert. And then Robert took out his own video camera and wanted to tape me. He asked for a superhero pose and I did one of my martial arts moves called a [kapueta kick]. And I have no idea how to spell that!" Taylor told the *Oregon Herald*. Taylor's "kapueta kick" did the trick, whether he could spell it or not. It's a complicated move, but, of course, Taylor could do it flawlessly, as he told the *Oregon Herald*, "I stand on one hand and I'm upside down and my legs are in a split position. And his son really liked that." Robert really liked Taylor, but it was Robert's son Racer who chose Taylor to play Sharkboy. "I guess Robert held up pictures of the kids that had callbacks and he said to Racer, 'Which one do you like?' He said, 'That one,' and pointed to me. And Robert said, 'That's what I was thinking.'" Taylor explained to the *Grand Rapids Press*. Racer was only eight years old at the time, but he already had incredible taste! Taylor couldn't have been happier when his agent called about a month after his callback with the good news—Taylor had won the part! "Oh, we freaked out," Taylor told the *Grand Rapids Press*. "My whole family couldn't sleep for, like, a week."

Taylor was even more excited about his new role when he read the entire script for *The Adventures of Sharkboy and Lavagirl*. "It's about a 10 year old named Max who doesn't fit in well in school. He gets picked on by bullies. And one day he dreams up two super heroes, Sharkboy and Lavagirl, while day dreaming in class. Eventually, Sharkboy and Lavagirl become real and they need Max to help them save their home world, a world which Max created. It's under destruction and being destroyed by Mr. Electric. And the film is about the series of adventures they have in order to save the planet and defeat Mr. Electric," Taylor told the *Oregon Herald*. Sharkboy and Lavagirl's world is called Planet Drool, and it's filled with imaginative places like the Land of Milk and Cookies, the Dream Graveyard, and the Ice Castle.

Sharkboy, Taylor's character, is a warrior with serious martial arts skills. "He's very self-confident and sometimes his confidence gets him into trouble—he starts fights and battles, and Lavagirl tries to cool him down. He's also kinda jealous of the character, Max, because he has an inside crush on Lavagirl and she's overly motherly to Max. And Sharkboy is also very acrobatic, so he uses lots of that in the fight scenes," Taylor told kidzworld.com. "[H]e was fun to play because he got to do a lot of acrobatic stuff. And he gets to move like a shark and throw lots and lots of temper tantrums!" Taylor told the *Oregon Herald*. It was a little bit of a challenge for Taylor to play such a hotheaded character, since Taylor himself is so easygoing, but he did a great job of making Sharkboy fierce, but still likable.

Cayden Boyd, who had guest starred on several television shows and in some movies like *Dodgeball: A True Underdog Story* and *Freaky Friday*, played Max. And Taylor Dooley was cast as Lavagirl. Taylor couldn't have been more excited—Taylor Dooley lived right across the street from him in Los Angeles! Lavagirl was her first role ever. Two other young actors, Jacob Davich and Sasha Pieterse, signed on as well. Jacob played Linus and Minus, and Sasha was Marissa Electricidad and the Ice Princess.

Comedian George Lopez was selected to play several roles including Mr. Electric, Mr. Electricidad, the Ice Guardian, and Tobor. *Sex and the City* actress Kristin Davis was cast as Max's mother, and famous funnyman David Arquette played Max's dad.

The kids really bonded with Robert Rodriguez, probably because he treated them like equals and friends. Most directors don't spend much time with the child stars in their movies when they aren't filming, but not Robert! "What's so amazing about Robert is that he directs his films, he writes them, he edits them, and he's even the cameraman. Best of all, he's a terrific pizza maker. He makes the best pizza! In his house, he has this big, stone oven. It's about 15 feet tall and he makes the most incredible pizza and ravioli!" Taylor told the *Oregon Herald*. "Everybody loved working with him. He played video games with us on the set. For instance, while I'd be shooting a particular scene, he'd be off playing video games with Taylor [Dooley]. It was so much fun." All in all, Taylor had a pretty phenomenal experience on his first movie. It was a lot of work, but it was also very rewarding.

Of course, playing a superhero wasn't all fun and games. "For *Sharkboy*, I was in the hair and makeup trailer for like 45 minutes every day and then wardrobe for a half hour. I had to get my whole suit on and everything. It was definitely a lot longer to get ready for *Sharkboy* because I'm playing a superhero. For *Sharkboy*, it's kind of harder to be in the moment because he's a superhero, and I'm not really a superhero. It was pretty easy, but playing a normal kid in real life is a lot easier," Taylor explained to ultimatedisney.com.

Once he had his costume on and his makeup and hair done, Taylor could really get into character, and he brought a lot of his own touches to Sharkboy. Robert and his son had created a great basic character, but Taylor got to decide what Sharkboy's attitude would be and even contribute some of the things he would say and do. As he told ultimatedisney.com, ". . . usually you get breakdowns and it says what your character is like and Robert Rodriguez just wanted us to create our own characters. He didn't want to put anything on a breakdown. So when you see the breakdown, it says 'Create your own.'

I just thought that Sharkboy would be whatever I wanted him to be, and I did that, and I guess Robert liked it."

Taylor's friends and family could definitely see bits of Taylor in Sharkboy when they watched the movie, and there were a few times where it seemed like it was more Taylor than Sharkboy on the screen! "I'm very sarcastic like Sharkboy, I think. A line that I have in the movie that's totally me is when our Train of Thought crashes into the mountain in the Land of Milk and Cookies and we land on the giant cookie, and Max is like 'Sharkboy, what happens when your Train of Thought wrecks?' And I'm like 'Well, can't be good, buddy.' I thought that was totally me. And also another thing is the acrobatic stuff that I do, like the martial arts. I did that in real life and then Robert found out about it and he asked me to choreograph my own fight scene," Taylor said to ultimatedisney.com. Taylor's martial arts and stunts choreography was top-notch, and he really impressed Robert with his ability to move for the camera. "Yes, I did my own stunts. When you see me doing the karate stuff and the fighting, that's what I do," Taylor explained to ultimatedisney.com.

Once the movie was finished, Taylor eagerly awaited its arrival in theaters. It must have been absolutely thrilling to know your work was going to be up on the big screen for millions of people to see. And when the big day finally arrived, the fans certainly weren't disappointed! They *loved* the finished film. And Taylor was just as thrilled to get to go to his premiere. "Well, the first time I saw it was at a cast and crew screening. It wasn't as different as I thought it would be. But it was fun watching how much fun we had on the set and how it turned out as a movie. It made me think of all the memories and moments from all the different scenes we shot. Previously, I'd done the red carpet five times before, attending the premieres of *Sahara, Sisterhood of the Traveling Pants*, and *Ladder 49*. But walking the red carpet, you wouldn't believe how many photographers are there! 'Taylor, turn over here. Turn to the right. Hold it here. To the left. Now over here.' It's really crazy on the red carpet, but knowing that it was your premiere made it even more fun," Taylor told the *Oregon Herald*.

That was Taylor's first real experience as a movie star, and he couldn't wait to do more! After all, who wouldn't want to walk the red carpet, hang out with other stars, and get paid to act in movies? And once the movie had been out for a little while, fans began to recognize Taylor everywhere he went. "Ten-year-old boys were the ones who first recognized me," Taylor told the *Grand Rapids Press*. "I'd be in the store, and boys would whisper to their moms. Then the moms would say, 'Excuse me—are you Sharkboy?'" Taylor was flattered that fans recognized him and wanted to meet him. "I just thought it was so cool," Taylor continued to the *Grand Rapids Press*. "I couldn't believe people wanted my picture." His fans' support made Taylor more eager than ever to continue down his path toward stardom.

In 2008, Taylor took another step along that path when he was cast as a regular on a new television show, NBC's *My Own Worst Enemy*. The show was about a mild-mannered consultant named Henry Spivey who lives with his wife Angie and their two children, Jack and Ruthy, in a Los Angeles suburb. But Henry has a second personality, Edward Albright, a master spy for a top secret government agency called the Janus Collective. Neither Edward nor Henry knows about the other, and Henry's family doesn't suspect a thing—when Janus needs Edward they summon Henry, switch him off, switch Edward on, and send Edward on his mission. Afterward they switch him back to Henry, who never realizes he was gone. But when something goes wrong on one of Edward's missions, he begins to switch between his two personalities at random, putting both of his lives and his family in jeopardy. Edward and Henry must then work to protect Henry's family and find a way to control the switches again. Hollywood heavyweight Christian Slater played Henry and Edward. Christian starred on Broadway when he was only nine years old and made his film debut in 1985 in *The Legend of Billie Jean*, as a young hunk not unlike Taylor Lautner! He went on to star in television, plays, and tons of movies. NBC cast beautiful actress Mädchen Amick, best known for her role on David Lynch's TV series *Twin Peaks*, as Henry's wife, Angie. But they still needed to find two young actors to play their children. Bella Thorne, a talented young actress who had starred in a number of popular shows and movies, took the role of Ruthy Spivey. All that was missing was an actor to play Henry's son, Jack. Luckily, there was a young, talented actor with all of the skills they needed just waiting for such an opportunity—Taylor! His athletic physique, martial arts and sports skills, and talent as an actor made him perfect to play the son of a spy. On the show, Jack is fifteen years old and a popular athlete. He is the star soccer player on his high school's team and a relatively new mixed martial artist. "My character is a star varsity soccer player," Taylor told the *Grand Rapids Press.* "And I'm gonna be able to use some of my martial arts. It'll be cool."

Taylor was pretty psyched when he got the news that he had won the role of Jack. After all, it was his first role as a regular cast member on a primetime series, and the show was sure to get lots of attention in the entertainment world. Plus, he had the chance to work with Christian Slater, one of the most talented and versatile actors in Hollywood. Taylor's role wasn't that big, since most of the series focused on Christian Slater's characters, so he was able to fit in filming between working on other projects and going to auditions. "I film *My Own Worst Enemy* but that's only about two days a week," Taylor told about.com. Taylor would go in at the start of every week to do a read-through of the script with the rest of the cast, and then go in one day to film his scenes. He had a great time working on the set and he loved getting to see his scenes every week in prime time.

Unfortunately, *My Own Worst Enemy* never did as well in the ratings as everyone had hoped. Almost everyone who saw the show loved it, but not enough people tuned in to keep the show on the air. It was canceled after nine episodes. Taylor was extremely disappointed, but he also understood that cancellations are fairly common for new television shows, so he wasn't totally surprised. Taylor really liked starring in a television series and working on his character over a season's worth of episodes. It was a nice change from film to have months for his character to change and grow, and Taylor has said he would love to star in another television series soon.

But that dream was about to be put on hold for the time being—for a major part in a hit movie!

# CHAPTER 14
# Up for the Role

On June 2, 2003, a woman named Stephenie Meyer had a dream. It was about a human girl and a vampire who loved her but hungered for her blood at the same time. Meyer was a writer, and she developed this dream into a novel, which she then sold to Little, Brown and Company, along with two sequels, for $750,000! The first book, *Twilight*, was released in 2005.

The response was immediate, and tremendous. *Twilight* won a number of book awards, including Publishers Weekly's Best Book of the Year and the *New York Times*'s Editor's Choice. The first sequel to *Twilight*, and the second book in the four-part series, *New Moon*, hit number 1 on the *New York Times* Best Sellers list in its second week. By the time the third book, *Eclipse*, came out, the series had spent a total of 143 weeks on the Best Sellers list! The fourth and final book in the series, *Breaking Dawn*, did great as well! The books have now sold over 42 million copies worldwide, and have been translated into thirty-seven different languages, making both *Twilight* and Stephenie Meyer household names.

Naturally, with success like that, a movie deal was not far behind.

It wasn't a smooth process, however Stephenie was very particular about the script, because *Twilight's* vampires aren't like the usual bloodsuckers of legend: They can go out in sunlight, they don't have fangs, and they never need to sleep, in dirt or otherwise. She turned down several offers and axed one deal before finally agreeing to a deal with Summit Entertainment. Melissa Rosenberg (who worked extensively in television and wrote the movies *Step Up* and *Alyx*) wrote a screenplay Stephenie was happy with, and Catherine Hardwicke (who had previously directed *Thirteen* and *Lords of Dogtown*) was selected to direct.

Then came the issue of casting.

Jackson didn't know anything about the Twilight series at first. He hadn't read any of the books, either, though he assured *Vanity Fair* that "many friends of mine had and filled me in on the story." And once he was cast for the first film, he made sure to pick up a copy of *Twilight*. As he explained to *Portrait* magazine, ". . . once I got the role, I read the first book. I haven't read the others on purpose because I didn't want to get ahead of my character. It's important to stay within the character and not get ahead of the story, although I did use Wikipedia to get some back story." So how was his audition? "It wasn't too bad," he told *Portrait*. "I actually lived really close to the audition and I had car troubles during the time so I just walked with my guitar. The other actors auditioning let me play my guitar so it was okay." Jackson likes to play guitar at auditions, so playing probably helped calm him down—and ultimately helped him win the role!

Jackson got cast as Jasper, one of the Cullen vampires. Jasper is the most recent addition to the Cullen family, and is still having difficulty getting used to the idea that he cannot simply feed on humans. "He's a vampire barely able to control himself, but he does it for love," Jackson told *Vanity*

*Fair*. Jackson could definitely relate to his character's sense of honor. Plus, both Jackson and Jasper are from Texas! Each of the vampires has a particular gift, and Jasper has the ability to alter people's emotions, though that isn't touched on much in the first book or movie.

Of course, Jasper is also something Jackson isn't: blond. But that didn't pose a problem. Far from it— Jackson told teenmag.com that "I really enjoyed it. I was always a character actor when I was in theatre. I kind of find that it helps the audience, especially with Jasper. I mean I'm not actually blonde so I had to bleach my hair blonde. I'm fairly pale. I'm more of an indoor sports kind of guy. I'm a musician so I spent most of my time awake at night and in the recording studio tucked away from the sun."

Not that changing his looks didn't cause a few issues. "The hair, the hair, the hair," Jackson told MTV.com. "Oh my God. See, there was a problem the first time they did the hair, that first press release. I don't know; there was some confusion over how to do it. We have a lot of producers, and we have a lot of input coming from all different directions, and so they decided to straighten my hair. My hair's naturally curly. It's also naturally brown, so they dyed my hair for the part. They tried straightening it, and it came out looking awful." Later they agreed to keep the curls, which worked much better, but Jackson still laughs about those early pictures.

Like his costar and on-screen brother, Jackson, Kellan hadn't read the books, either. "I didn't even know there was a book series," he admitted to *Vanity Fair*. "I read the script while I was in Africa and fell in love with it. I loved the vampire story. It felt so new and fresh, not the typical 'let's kill the vampire with a pitchfork' idea. It was really unique. They first sent me out for Edward's role, and as much as I would have loved to be the lead, it wasn't possible for me to fly back from Africa where I was shooting and audition as many times as they would have needed me to. So I read Emmett and he seemed so cool. Once I was cast, I was flown out to Oregon to start shooting, and my friend [and castmate] Ashley Greene had all of the books. She asked me if I had read the books, and I was like, 'Ha ha, you're joking.

There are no books.' So she gave them to me and I did my homework. I read all three of them. The fourth wasn't out yet."

That didn't mean it was easy to land the role, though! "Well I was actually . . . in Africa when the script for *Twilight* was released and they began to cast the film," Kellan revealed to snmag.com. "I tried to put myself on tape to send to my agent in LA. Well, I had the hardest time putting myself on tape due to our shooting schedule [for *Generation Kill*], as well as not having all the needed resources, so time came and went and soon enough *Twilight* was cast. I finished shooting *Generation Kill* right before Christmas of 2007. I had been away from home for seven months shooting in Africa and really just wanted a vacation. That's what I told my team and they respected that. Then my agent called me and told me they re-opened the role of Emmett due to unknown reasons and said it must be fate and got me the appointment. I went to the audition and they liked what I did and wanted to fly me out to Portland to read for director Catherine Hardwicke. So off I went to Portland and once there, I met

Catherine, read for her, and got the part."

Surprisingly, casting the female lead of Bella proved very easy. Director Catherine Hardwicke had seen Kristen Stewart in Sean Penn's *Into the Wild* the previous year, and told *Entertainment Weekly* that "her mixture of innocence and longing just knocked me out." She sent Kristen the *Twilight* script the second she had it in hand, then flew from L.A. to Pittsburgh to meet with her—Kristin was there filming the movie *Adventureland*. "She'd been shooting all night, but she learned her lines on the spot," Catherine recounted to *Entertainment Weekly*. "She danced on the bed and chased pigeons in the park. I was captivated." Catherine had found her Bella.

Then came the issue of casting the male lead, vampire Edward Cullen. That was a bit more difficult. "Everybody has such an idealized vision of Edward," Catherine told *Entertainment Weekly*. "[The book's fans] were rabid. Like, old ladies saying, 'You better get it right.'" She thought Robert Pattinson might fit the bill, but wasn't entirely convinced until he flew out to see her in Venice,

California, and she made him audition then and there with Kristen Stewart. The result? "The room shorted out," Catherine told *Entertainment Weekly*. "The sky opened up, and I was like, 'This is going to be good.'" On December 11, 2007, Summit Entertainment revealed that Robert Pattinson would be starring opposite Kristen Stewart. *Twilight*'s author Stephenie Meyer had originally wanted Henry Cavill (who played Albert Mondego in *The Count of Monte Cristo* and Melot in *Tristan & Isolde*) to play Edward, but by the time the movie was being cast he was twenty-five and considered too old to play a seventeen-year-old—even an immortal vampire who barely looked seventeen! But once she heard about Robert's stellar audition, Stephenie agreed that he was perfect. She posted the news on her blog, saying, "I am ecstatic with Summit's choice for Edward. There are very few actors who can look both dangerous and beautiful at the same time, and even fewer who I can picture in my head as Edward. Robert Pattinson is going to be amazing."

Not everyone agreed, however. A lot of fans

had their own idea of what Edward looked like, and Robert definitely wasn't it! He had a tough road ahead if he was going to prove to everyone that Catherine had made the right choice. But Robert was up to the task!

Taylor Lautner didn't know much about *Twilight* when he booked the audition, but once he learned a little more, he felt like he was perfect for the part. "I realized how big it was," Taylor told the *Grand Rapids Press*. "Suddenly, it was all over the Internet. I started hearing about all the hype, all the fans. I thought, 'Oh my goodness. If I get this, it'll be huge.' I realized I really want this." He had the dark good looks and physical skills to play the rough and tumble werewolf Jacob, and he had the heritage, as he told MTV.com, ". . . actually, I am part Native American. We learned that through [preparing for] this film. I'm French, Dutch and German, and on my mother's side, she has some Potawatomi and Ottawa Indian in her."

Taylor might have looked the part, but he also had to prove to the directors that he had believable romantic chemistry with costar Kristen Stewart.

"I originally met with Catherine and she wanted me to do a 'chemistry read' with Kristen Stewart. We did a few scenes from the first book, like the beach scene, and then we read some lines straight out of the books 'New Moon' and 'Eclipse,'" Taylor explained to the *Los Angeles Times* blog. Next, Taylor had to show them that he could play Jacob as he grew from a regular kid into a more troubled, lovesick young man. Taylor had been practicing and he was ready! "I don't remember the specific scenes, but I do know that the scenes I did showed a huge difference in Jacob's character. He goes from happy-go-lucky and friendly in 'Twilight' to when he's more of a werewolf and more of an adult, all intense and grumpy. She wanted to see as much of me playing the different sides to Jacob as possible," Taylor explained to the *Los Angeles Times* blog. Clearly he impressed Catherine, and she finally offered him the role!

Finally, casting was complete! Jackson, Kellan, Robert, and Taylor were all on board, along with Kristen as Bella, Billy Burke as her father, Sheriff Charlie Swan, Ashley Greene as Alice Cullen, Nikki

Reed as Rosalie Hale, Peter Facinelli as Dr. Carlisle Cullen, and Cam Gigandet as James, among others. The wait was over—it was time to start filming!

# CHAPTER 15
## *Twilight*

Catherine Hardwicke had selected the area in and around Portland, Oregon, for filming, but she didn't bring the entire cast out there—not at first. As Jackson told *Portrait* magazine, "Well at first it was just the vampires on set because we were practicing stunts and preparing for the big fight scene. So when the humans came, we were all like what, humans?? But after a day we all started hanging out and became really close. It was great though because we were a large young cast so we could all go out and have fun."

"The cast really had great chemistry and we all hung out," Taylor agreed when he spoke to *Vanity Fair*. "We're all really good friends now, so that's really cool." There was a lot of fun, a lot of silliness—and a lot of music. "I believe there are usually two or three guitars on set at all times," Jackson revealed to radaronline.com. "We all get down with a little music, though some of our styles and tastes are a bit different."

Taylor was a little nervous at first, since he was the youngest member of the cast. He was sixteen during filming, and he must have been a little afraid that the rest of the cast wouldn't be willing to hang out with a teenager. "At first I was a little bit nervous about that but if you think about it, I'm only a year and a half younger than Kristen [Stewart]. But the cast is really friendly and we all had great chemistry and we all got along. I honestly don't feel the age difference," Taylor told Celebrity News Service. Taylor felt right at home with his new friends, and they spent lots of time together on and off the set. "Yeah, the cast is awesome. And the thing I think the fans are going to like the most is that the cast has such great chemistry—Rob and Kristen, the whole cast. Portland, where we filmed, has the best food I've ever had. So most of our time, we wake up bright and early, go film until 6 o'clock at night, so all we had time for was go back, get a bite to eat together, and hit the hay for the next day. So it was quite fun, though, the cast is awesome," Taylor said to alloy.com. Most of Taylor's scenes occurred with just Kristen, so he bonded with her the most. "The only people that were there when I was on set were Kristen and Rob, and he wasn't there too much. So it was basically just me and Kristen. She's very easygoing. It takes her a little bit to warm up to people. She's a little shy and reserved. Her and Rob both are. But she was very fun to be around," Taylor explained to the *Los Angeles Times* blog.

Kellan had some concerns of his own about fitting in, but not because of his age—he was the last person cast, and didn't want to be left out. But there was something else working to his advantage. "I've been so fortunate to work with a lot of my friends," he told *Vanity Fair*. "I knew Jackson Rathbone [Jasper] and Ashley Greene [Alice] before we started, but I was a late-comer on the film. I booked Emmett on one of the last days of rehearsal, so I definitely came in as the new guy. That's always tough, but having good friends that I already knew made it much easier. The whole cast is really great, and I'm so excited to do the rest of the series with them. We're still really close and we all still hang out."

Of course, all of the actors had individual challenges as well. Like Robert, when it came to the baseball scene. "He sucks at anything athletic," Kellan laughingly told about.com. "He cannot throw a ball and run. Like it's funny, we had a running scene in the movie and I can't believe how much faster I am than him. And by the time I'd got to where we had to get, I'd turn around and I'd see him trying to run. Like I've never seen someone try to run." Robert agreed. "I'm atrociously unfit," he said when talking to the Associated Press. "Every tiny little stunt takes it out of me. I think I pulled my hamstring on the first stunt of the first day just trying to pick Bella up and she weighs about 100 pounds." Robert was a quick learner, though—his athletic scenes in the movie look flawless!

Jackson had problems with the baseball scene, too, but for a completely different reason. "For the baseball scene, they made me bat with my left hand," he explained to *Portrait*. "I'm not a leftie at all so I looked ridiculous doing it! It was pretty embarrassing . . . but I finally got it down at the end!"

Kellan's own issue was something much smaller—in size. "I loved playing a vampire," he assured *Vanity Fair*, "but it was really tough because I don't wear contacts. Just putting in those contacts would take me 45 minutes to an hour. We had a makeup artist named Jeannie who, bless her heart, would put them in for me everyday. Eventually we got it down to only taking five minutes."

Taylor's problem on the set was also related to his appearance. "When I first heard that I was going to be wearing a wig I was really excited," he told teenmag.com. "I was like 'Cool, I have never worn a wig before, this is going to be fun change my look up a bit.' But then, after the first day of filming I was through with it. It was really itchy, it was always getting in my face! I'd be trying to eat lunch and it's in my mouth and, yeah, even when were filming the scenes and I'm talking and it's in my mouth and agh! It was quite the adventure with the wig."

Location and weather were also big concerns for the cast and crew. Initially, First Beach in LaPush, Oregon, was planned as the site of the critical beach scene where Bella first hears the legends of Forks and its people, particularly the "cold ones" she later realizes are the Cullen vampires. Most of the movie was shot in Portland and in St. Helens, however, and ultimately the producers decided LaPush was simply too far away to be feasible as a location. Then there was the weather itself. The movie is set in Forks, Washington, for a reason—vampires, even Stephenie Meyer's version, don't like the sun. Hardwicke and the producers thought Oregon would have the perfect weather for their needs—it is the Pacific Northwest, after all. But the sun kept coming out during filming! They had to resort to fake rain several times, including some of the high-school classroom scenes. As Jackson told *Portrait* magazine, "We had to film when it was overcast, especially during the school scenes, so when the sun came out, we would have to run to the second set (we would have a cover set to use when it became sunny) so there was a lot of running around! We had to figure out which set we were going to be at for more than an hour because the weather kept changing so drastically."

The weather also refused to cooperate

for the baseball scene. "In I guess the second month of shooting we were doing the baseball stuff down in the gorge," Kellan related to twilightcocoa.blogspot.com. "And the weather was just so insane. Everyone was like, alright lets just do this, let's play baseball and get this scene done. I love rain, I love hail, and I love snow and that's what it did every thirty minutes. We would set up and shoot and it would start hailing! Like huge pieces of ice would come down. It was just a funny predicament. So we would go into the holding tents and wait for it to stop. Then go and start to set up again and as soon as we would start to film it would start raining. We had a crane up and a black out cloth, and it caught the rain. So when we moved the crane once it dumped all the water on this one AD. He was cool about it. But I just loved that day because the weather was so cool and everyone hated it so it made me laugh."

Everything worked out in the end, though. The filming finished more or less on schedule, the movie went into postproduction, and everything was on track for the movie's premiere on November 21,

2008. The fans couldn't wait—and neither could Jackson, Kellan, Robert, and Taylor!

# CHAPTER 16
## All That Glitters

The guys and the rest of the *Twilight* cast knew that the movie would be big, but nothing could have prepared them for just how big it ended up being. Fans of the books couldn't wait to see the movie, and many of them ended up seeing it multiple times. Shows sold out days in advance of each screening, and some fans even came dressed up as their favorite characters or in *Twilight* T-shirts just to watch it in the theater! The movie debuted at number 1 at the box office and brought in $70 million its opening weekend, making it the highest debut for a female director, and the highest ever non-summer, non-sequel debut. *Twilight* grossed over $340 million worldwide in its first three months. And in June 2009, the film won several coveted MTV Movie Awards, including Best Movie, Best Female Performance (for Kristen Stewart), Breakthrough

Performance Male (for Robert Pattinson), and Best Kiss (for Kristen and Robert).

It wasn't just the movie that was getting a lot of attention, though. So were its stars—especially the leads, Robert and Kristen! "I asked the producer, 'Is Rob ready for this? Have you guys prepped him? Is he ready to be the It Guy?'" *Twilight* author Stephenie Meyer told *Entertainment Weekly* when they were preparing to do their second *Twilight*-themed issue on November 14, 2008, which featured Robert on one of three collectible covers. "I don't think he really is. I don't think he sees himself that way. And I think the transition is going to be a little rocky." Of course, Robert takes a very mature view toward his newfound stardom. He told people.com he'd learned something very important from his first big role as Cedric Diggory in *Harry Potter*: "Having it die down afterwards. Having it being the hot thing for a few months and then it just going . . . It helps. It helps once you get used to it and know that no one will care. Once you're immune to failure, it's like nothing matters." Still, that didn't stop Rob from admitting to thestar.com, "It's absolutely nuts. It's just crazy. A year ago I couldn't get a date and now the whole world's turned over."

The other three boys were also getting a lot of unexpected attention. Jackson was a little more concerned about it than Rob, not because he didn't think he could handle the fame but because he didn't want such a sudden increase in attention and exposure. "I hope it's not going to change too much," he told Bloody Disgusting TV about his life while on the set for his upcoming film *Dread*. "I've been blessed to have this film and it's brought me a lot of other opportunities. It brought me [*Dread*], *S. Darko*, and *The Last Airbender*. Our band [100 Monkeys] has been taking off. People have been paying a lot more attention to us, which is fantastic. We haven't even finished our album so it's kind of like 'Wow.' It's a great launching point—I'm really grateful for it. But at the same time, I like the gradual career process that I've had. And in many ways, it's kind of going to stay that way. I don't want this jet rocket to stardom or anything."

Kellan, however, was a bit more relaxed about the whole "fame" issue. "There have been so many funny stories!" he told *Saturday Night* magazine. "I live next to a high school and my roommates had a fun idea to go and check out the local high-school football game and just hang and watch a game and eat stadium food. So a group of us went to the game and as soon as I bought my ticket, my buddy got the feeling that someone was following us. He was right. As soon as we got to the hot dog stand, this girl said 'Kellan I love you. Can I have a picture?' She was shaking so much which I thought it was very cute and of course we talked for a bit and took some pictures and we said goodbye. We finally got our food and found seats and all of a sudden groups of kids kept coming up to our seats asking for pictures and autographs and wanting me to sign everything from their jeans to their shoes. It was funny and very flattering; I was barely able to watch the game. I guess I should have thought twice about it being a high school football game . . . but still, it was a fun night. The fan attention's fun and I'm very flattered. Everyone I have met has been so kind and sweet. We know what big fans of *Twilight* they are so we just want to please them as much as we can."

Taylor got his first real taste of just how devoted his new fans were when he and the rest of the cast appeared at Comic-Con in San Diego in the summer of 2008 before *Twilight* even hit theaters! Comic-Con is an annual convention to promote comic books and all things supernatural in the entertainment world. *Twilight* fans were there in droves, hoping to get a sneak peek of anything having to do with the movie, and they weren't disappointed. "We were all standing backstage waiting to go out and they told me 'It's going to be crazy. Once you get downstairs there's going to be 6,500 fans.' I kind of brushed it off and said 'Yeah, OK, sure.' But then *Twilight* came up on the screen, and everyone just started screaming. I've never seen anything like it before. We were all pretty nervous but once we got out there it was pretty fun—at least for me. The fans are just very passionate and really excited for the movie to come out already. So am I!" Taylor explained to the *Los Angeles Times* blog. Of all of the *Twilight* stars, Taylor handled Comic-Con the best. He's always been outgoing, so he loved meeting the fans and getting them pumped up for the movie. Kristen and Robert, however, are both pretty shy, so they were a little overwhelmed with all of the attention and had to ask Taylor for advice! "Actually, both [Robert] and Kristen have come up to me and asked, 'How do you not freak out? What do you do?' And they're all sweating. I tell them, 'I don't know. I mean, this is fun!' But they're all disappointed, like 'Oh, OK.' They're funny," Taylor explained to the *Los Angeles Times* blog.

One of the biggest *Twilight*-related phenomena has to do with Rob and Taylor's characters, Edward and Jacob. *Twilight* fans have been pretty evenly divided about who they want to end up with Bella since the books first came out. Some fans want Jacob and Bella together and others want Edward and Bella together. Fans of the movie are just as evenly divided into "Team Jacob" and "Team Edward." Of course, only one team got their way, but you'll have to read *Breaking Dawn* or wait for the fourth movie to find out! Team Jacob and Team Edward members can buy all sorts of merchandise featuring Jacob Black or Edward Cullen, like T-shirts, journals, and even underwear! But that's not all; there are even a few places where you can get merchandise based on the actors themselves! "Well, one of the weirdest and scariest things that I've discovered is that there is underwear—women's underwear—being sold on the Internet and it has 'Team Taylor' written on it," Taylor explained to the *Los Angeles Times* blog. "Women's underwear is being sold with my name [not Jacob's] imprinted on the front of it. One of my friends or family members e-mailed me the link and asked 'What is this?' I'm not quite sure." Taylor is a little embarrassed about having his name on underwear, but he's also flattered. Just don't ask him to sign it—he'd turn bright red! But at the end of the day, the *Twilight* boys know that this sort of thing is all a part of being famous, and they try to take it in stride. The most important thing to them is making their fans happy. And the fans have plenty to be happy about, with three more *Twilight* movies to look forward to!

# CHAPTER 17

# The Moon Shines Bright

Of course, the question all *Twilight* fans really want answered is what the future holds for the films. The first film was such a huge success that the sequel, *New Moon*, was quickly green-lit. Catherine Hardwicke had a scheduling conflict, however, so she reluctantly stepped down from directing the second movie and was replaced by Chris Weitz. "I've seen a few of [Chris Weitz's] films, and he's really talented," Taylor told MTV.com. "The same thing with Catherine [Hardwicke]; I mean, Catherine had a really interesting mind. [Weitz] has that as well, and he's very talented. I've heard a lot of good stuff about him, so I'm excited to meet him. I heard he's like a surfer dude, and that he's really laid-back and friendly. It'll be fun." Robert thought so as well. "He's a great guy," Rob told fandango.com when talking about Weitz. "He's very, very talented, and articulate.

I guess it must be kind of stressful for him to take this on. It's got so much expectation. He just seems very calm about everything." Weitz is best known for writing and directing both the touching Hugh Grant movie *About a Boy* (which was adapted from the book by Nick Hornby) and the sweeping fantasy movie *The Golden Compass* (which was adapted from a Philip Pullman novel of the same name).

Robert, Kristen, and many of the other cast members were quickly signed on to reprise their roles for the rest of the film. "Wait, there's another one?" Jackson joked when *Inked* magazine asked in May 2009 if he had been signed for *New Moon*. "Just kidding. Yes, I'm on board. I actually go up to Toronto to start training in a few days." Kellan was quickly signed on as well, though he claimed when talking to about.com that he didn't know—or couldn't say—if he'd been signed for two movies originally or for four (there are four books in the Twilight series).

One of the actors, however, wasn't as certain that he'd be asked to repeat his role in the second film—Taylor. "I think it's because, well, Rob and

Kristen were the lead roles in *Twilight*, so they've got to be back," Taylor told MTV.com. "I don't even know if they're officially signed; maybe they are, I don't know. They just hired Weitz, and now they're just moving down the cast. All I can say is, I'm going to be ready if my number's called."

Taylor wanted to continue on as Jacob, but the producers were concerned that Taylor didn't look old enough or big enough to play Jacob in the future films. Taylor is about 5'9" and very muscular, but in *New Moon*, Jacob shoots up to 6'5" and gains lots of muscle when he becomes a werewolf. Jacob is supposed to be fierce, intimidating, and very manly, and the producers were worried that baby-faced Taylor wouldn't look big and bad enough. But Taylor has always had confidence that he can make anything work. "In the first one, [Jacob] is just regular and lanky and not crazy," Taylor told MTV.com. "But I'm sure after this one, I will be working out, eating my protein, and staying away from the ice cream and the sugar." He was already in great shape, but as soon as filming for *Twilight* wrapped, Taylor began working out and quickly gained some serious extra muscle. "I have been working out. I've been working out since the day we finished filming *Twilight*. I just weighed myself today; I've put on nineteen pounds," Taylor told MTV.com. When rumors began swirling that Taylor might not be recast, his agent set up a meeting with the director and producers, and Taylor worked hard to prepare for that meeting. Taylor told MTV.com, "I'm guaranteeing Weitz 10 more [pounds] by filming. I get to meet Chris on Friday, in two days, so I'm excited. I'm going to have lunch with him."

Taylor's fans rallied around their favorite actor, posting on message boards, signing petitions, and doing everything they could to show Summit Entertainment that they will not accept any other actor as Jacob. Taylor appreciated the support, and just tried not to worry and to focus on preparing for the role. "My job for *Twilight* was to bring Jacob to life—the friendly, happy-go-lucky little Jacob," Taylor explained to MTV.com. "And my job for *New Moon* is completely different; I've been looking forward to that. I've been getting ready for it, and I can assure them that I will follow through with that job." Luckily Chris Weitz knew he had a good thing in Taylor and signed him on to play Jacob in all of the *Twilight* movies! The other guys were thrilled as well—as Kellan told the *Los Angeles Times* blog, "Taylor's going to be great. He's really stepped up to the role and he deserves it."

*New Moon* was also filmed in the Northwest, but this time the producers and the director opted for a slightly different spot. They chose Pacific Rim National Park Reserve in Canada, and were apparently pleased with their selection—and with its weather. "The weather is perfect for us: rainy, dismal, in the sense of the visuals, the mist on the ocean, the cloudiness, the erratic wind activity," *New Moon's* coproducer Bill Bannerman told the *Canadian Press.* "Everything is exactly what it should be." The first scenes were shot on the reserve's rocky South Beach, but later scenes took place on Incinerator Rock at Long Beach. Most of the area locals were excited about having the movie there. "This is a project that we're thrilled to have in our region," Vancouver Island North Film Commissioner Joan Miller told ctv.ca. "We worked on [getting] the first movie but because the Canadian dollar got so strong we lost it to Oregon. With the position the Canadian dollar is in right now, we've been able to have another kick at the can, and we've been successful. So here it is."

*New Moon* wrapped filming in May 2009, and fans seem just as excited about this movie as they were about *Twilight*. The two films will definitely have their differences, however. As Robert told fandango.com, "The interesting thing about this one is that so much of my character is in Bella's head. It's based on a mixture of memories and nightmares. Bella thinks she is going mad. I get to do some really creepy stuff. In other words, Bella is really frightened of [her hallucinations]. It's really, really different than *Twilight*. I think that a lot of people will be kind of scared by this one. I wanted to try and put that into *Twilight* but I couldn't really find a way to make Edward scary."

Jackson has a much bigger role to play in the second movie as well, and his character Jasper has a critical scene early on. "I don't want to reveal much," he insisted when asked by foforks.com, "but I must assure the fans that Melissa is an incredible screenwriter, and the movies are only going to get better." That's a bold statement, considering how well *Twilight* did! But clearly we'll just have to wait and see. At least we know Jackson, Kellan, Robert, and Taylor will all be in the other films, so we have that to look forward to!

# CHAPTER 18

## After *New Moon*

So what did Jackson, Kellan, Robert, and Taylor do between *Twilight* and *New Moon* (other than prep for the second movie)? And what are they doing now that *New Moon* has finished shooting? Well, all four of them have kept busy, that's for sure!

After *Twilight*, Jackson moved on to another eerie film—and, as if mentally preparing himself for *New Moon*, it was another sequel! He took the role of Jeremy in *S. Darko*, a follow-up to the cult classic *Donnie Darko*. Released in 2001, *Donnie Darko* starred Jake Gyllenhaal (best known for this role and for his Oscar-nominated turn in *Brokeback Mountain*) as the title character, a troubled young man whose world begins to change around him after a damaged plane engine crashes through his room and almost kills him. *S. Darko* is set seven years later and follows Donnie's younger sister Samantha (played by Daveigh Chase, who played the same role in the first movie and who also starred as Rhonda Volmer on *Big Love*), who decides to flee her home with her best friend Corey (played by Briana Evigan from *Step Up 2: The Streets*) and head to Los Angeles to look for new experiences. They wind up in the town of Conejo Springs, which is an unusual place filled with odd characters. Jackson plays Jeremy, the town nerd, who falls for Samantha upon first sight. Bizarre events begin to unfold around Samantha, just as they did to her brother, and she and Corey struggle to make sense of it all. *S. Darko* was released on May 12, 2009.

One movie wasn't enough to keep Jackson occupied, however—not with all his energy! So after *S. Darko*, he appeared in *Dread*, a movie about three college students who set out to discover and document what people dread the most. Jackson plays Stephen Grace, while Shaun Evans (of *Teachers*, *Being Julia*, and *Gone*) plays Quaid and Hanne Steen (Carmel from *Ideal*) plays Cheryl Fromm. The movie is based on a Clive Barker short story, which was adapted and directed by Anthony DiBlasi, who produced Barker's movies *The Plague, Book of Blood,* and *The Midnight Meat Train. Dread* had an early screening on May 5, 2009, and will be officially released some time in 2009. "We're definitely not making 'I Know What You Did 3 Summers Ago' or anything like that," Jackson told shocktillyoudrop.com. "When you get down to it, we all feel dread and we all have reasons for what inspired it. That's what we're trying to get to the root of in this film. The imagery in this film is haunting, stuff that's made a lot of people sick."

And Jackson's already got another project going now that *New Moon* has wrapped! His next role is in the live-action film *The Last Airbender.* It's based on the animated series *Avatar,* which is set in a fantasy world ruled by four different nations: Fire, Air, Earth, and Water. Each tribe has people who can actually control their chosen element, known as Firebenders, Airbenders, Earthbenders, and Waterbenders. Then there is the Avatar, who has mastery over all four and who helps keep the tribes in balance. When the Avatar disappears, the warlike Fire Nation is quick to attack the others and dominate them. A hundred years pass before a pair of young Water Nation kids, Sokka and Katara, find a boy frozen in the ice. His name is Aang, and he is the Avatar! But so much time has passed—Aang was only partway through his training in his native Airbending, and has no experience whatsoever with the other three elements. Can he and his new friends find a way for him to learn those other elements and defeat the Fire Nation to bring the world back into balance? In the live-action version, Jackson plays Sokka, the young Water Nation warrior who's a bit too full of himself and a bit too impressed with his own skills but who has a good heart. Nicola Peltz of *Deck the Halls* and *Harold* plays his sister, the apprentice Waterbender Katara, and newcomer Noah Ringer plays Aang. Dev Patel from the Oscar winning movie *Slumdog Millionaire* plays the Fire Nation prince Zuko, who is obsessed with finding Aang and delivering him to his father, the Firelord Ozai (Cliff Curtis of *Whale Rider*, *Fracture*, *The Fountain*, and *Sunshine*), in chains. Jackson had a great time working on the movie—and doing the stunts! "I've been doing a lot of Kung Fu training," he told radaronline.com, "and I've had to do a good deal of fighting in the last few weeks. It's a lot of fun, but my band mates are tired of me trying to Kung Fu them before and after shows."

Kellan is a very physical guy, and really enjoyed the fight scenes in *Twilight*. Is it any wonder, then, that his next movie is titled *Warrior*? Kellan plays Conor Sullivan, a young hothead and star lacrosse player. When his marine father dies in combat, Conor starts acting out in self-destructive ways. His mom, Claire (*Burn Notice*'s Gabrielle Anwar), can't figure out how to reach him through his shock and grief—or her own. But Conor's dad's old combat buddy, Sargeant Major Duke Wayne (Adam Beach of *Windtalkers* and *Law & Order: Special Victims Unit*) takes Conor to a wilderness lacrosse camp, where Conor learns about maturity, sportsmanship, and the true meaning of manhood. The movie also stars William Mapother (*Lost*'s Ethan Rom) as Conor's lacrosse coach, David Milligan. Mapother had recently shot the movie *Hurt* with one of Kellan's pals, Jackson Rathbone! And one of Kellan's buddies and fellow *Twilight* actors joined him in *Warriors*—Ashley Greene, who plays Kellan's sister

Alice Cullen in *Twilight*. In *Warriors,* she plays the coach's daughter, Brooklyn, who becomes Conor's love interest. The two were friends before *Twilight,* and had a great time filming a second movie together. *Warriors* is expected to be released late in 2009.

Next, Kellan took part in the reinvention of a slasher classic. *A Nightmare on Elm Street* first hit the big screen in 1984. It starred Heather Langenkamp (who later starred as Marie Lubbock in *Just the Ten of Us*) as Nancy Thompson, a teenage girl who discovers that the street she lives on has a horrible past. Years before, a man named Freddy Krueger (played by veteran actor Robert Englund, who also appeared in *V, The Phantom of the Opera*, *Night Terrors*, *Nightmare Café*, and *Jack Brooks: Monster Slayer*) had lived there, and had kidnapped, tortured, and slaughtered the neighborhood children. He was known as the Springwood Slasher because he used a glove he had crafted himself, which had straight-razor blades affixed to the fingers. Krueger was ultimately caught and tried, but freed on a technicality. His victims' parents and their neighbors, outraged, hunted Krueger down. They found him in the boiler room where he worked and burned him alive, then agreed never to speak of it. But Freddy didn't die completely. Somehow he slipped into people's dreams instead, and there he continues to kill children—in their sleep. The original movie spawned an entire series and was a slasher phenomenon—it was also the first-ever role for a young man named Johnny Depp!

When top music video director Samuel Bayer, Eric Heisserer (who created the cult Internet sensation *Dionaea House*), and horror legend Wes Craven (who wrote many of the greatest slasher movies, including *The Hills Have Eyes* and the original *A Nightmare on Elm Street*) decided to recreate the original, Kellan was cast as Dean, one of Nancy's friends. And who's playing Freddy this time around? None other than Jackie Earle Haley, who first drew attention in *The Bad News Bears* and *Breaking Away* and got rave reviews in early 2009 for his role as the vigilante Rorschach in *Watchmen*. Are you scared yet?

While Kellan was busy doing action movies and horror films, Robert went a different route. His next film after *Twilight* was *The Summer House*, which is a dramatic short about a young man who follows his suddenly-ex-girlfriend to France in an attempt to get back together with her. It also stars Laurence Beck, Talulah Riley (who played Mary Bennet in *Pride & Prejudice* alongside Keira Knightley, and Annabelle Fritton in *St. Trinian's*), and three older veteran television and movie actors—Marianne Borgo, David Burke, and Anna Calder-Marshall—who have all been acting steadily since the 1960s. The short was written by Laurence's brother Ian Beck, who also wrote *Prisoner of War*. It debuted at the Cannes Film Festival on May 14, 2009, to rave reviews.

After *The Summer House*, Robert moved on to another unique project. He took the role of Art in *How to Be*, a quirky little film about a young man who convinces a Canadian self-help guru to move to London and live with his family and become his personal life coach. Jeremy Hardy, an actor best known for his roles on game and comedy shows like *Back in the Day*, *That'll Test 'Em*, *Countdown*, and *Batteries Not Included*, plays the guru Jeremy. Rebecca Pidgeon (Charlotte Ryan on *The Unit*) and Michael

Irving (Jayson from *Lou Grant*) play Art's confused parents. The director, Oliver Irving, told *People* how thrilled he was with Robert's performance. "He has a playfulness and naivety that he was able to inject into the character. He's very down to earth and unpretentious. I think that's probably what makes him appealing." *How to Be* was shown in Britain on June 20, 2009, at select locations. In the United States, it was available through IFC Festival Direct for three months, starting on April 29, 2009.

Next, Robert acted in the small art film *Little Ashes*, which tells the story of surrealist master painter Salvador Dalí and his close friends, the writer Federico García Lorca and filmmaker Luis Buñuel. And who does Robert play in the film? Why, Dalí himself! The movie also stars Javier Beltrán (who starred as Pep on the Spanish television series *Zoo*) as Federico García Lorca, Matthew McNulty (of *The Mark of Cain*, *Control*, and *Honest*) as Luis Buñuel, and Marina Gatell (who starred in the Spanish television series *7 vidas*, *Majoria absoluta*, *El mundo de Chema*, and many movies) as Margarita. The movie is set in 1922 in Madrid, Spain, and Dalí has just arrived to study art at the university there. He is drawn to Lorca and Buñuel and the three become a trio, setting styles and trends all around them. Eventually Dalí and Lorca become really close, and spend a holiday together in the seaside town of Cadaques, working on their art. "I just researched tons and tons of stuff because everyone spoke Spanish on the set and so I just read all day," Robert told about.com. "It was the first time that I ever really got into characterization, trying to work on movements. There was a photo of him pointing and I kept trying to figure out how he pointed for like three days. I've never done that for any job. I was doing tons of stuff on his walk and such. By the end, I have no idea [how it turned out]. Someone said to me the other day, 'I had no idea it was about Dalí until you had the mustache at the end.' I was just like, 'Oh, great.' I think it's a kind of homage to him, I guess, in that performance. I've never related to a character more than him, which is really weird because everyone thinks that he's some nut job. When he was younger, if you read his autobiographical stuff—he wrote three autobiographies which completely contradict each other . . . There are chapters called 'Truth' and other ones are called 'Lies' and then lies and the truths and stuff, it's just really funny. There was so much about him that I found fascinating. It's depressing how he did it himself and yet everyone sees him as this mask. He wanted that, but it's so funny how he was so much more than just this bizarre clown that he was at the end of his life who only cared about money. He was an incredibly complex person. I'm not saying that I am. I'm not at all." *Little Ashes* was released on May 8, 2009.

Taylor was busy working out in order to win back his role of Jacob Black for *New Moon*, so unlike the others he didn't film any additional movies between filming *Twilight* and *New Moon*. That's not likely to stop him for long, though. Taylor has a lot of focus—he loves acting, and he's not going to be letting go of it anytime soon. He's still going on auditions and looking for roles that will challenge him as an actor and help him on his path to stardom. But Taylor won't take just any role. He's not in a big hurry to grow up, so he wants to focus on taking roles that are age appropriate for him and his fans.

Taylor loves working on movies, but he also had a blast being on a television series and he's definitely up to do it again! He was psyched when he saw all of the cool action scenes in *My Own Worst Enemy*, and of course, Taylor is also hoping he can put his two loves—sports and acting—together at some point in the future. He would love to do action or sports movies where he could do his own stunts and maybe use his martial arts skills. Taylor really looks up to actors like Denzel Washington and Matt Damon, both of whom have proven that they can take on any type of role and deliver a flawless performance. Denzel is intense and passionate and Matt is funny and a great action star. Taylor is somewhere in between. He has the passion, focus, sense of humor, and action skills to ensure that his career will be as long and successful as his idols!

But it isn't just acting that Taylor loves. He'd also like to branch out and try his hand at directing someday. "I would love to go the acting route, but if I couldn't, I would want to be like Robert Rodriguez, a writer and director," Taylor told the *Oregon Herald* right after he filmed *The Adventures of Sharkboy and*

*Lavagirl.* Taylor's acting career has certainly taken off since then, but he hasn't given up on his dream of directing someday. But director might not be the only job he'd want to try. Taylor has had enough experience on film sets to learn a lot about what goes on behind the scenes, and he'd be a perfect fit for several different roles in the film industry. He choreographed his own martial arts scenes for *The Adventures of Sharkboy and Lavagirl,* and he is an expert when it comes to stunts. Taylor could work as a choreographer for fight and battle scenes, a stuntman, or he could train other actors and actresses to perform believable martial arts for roles. As he's already proven, Taylor can achieve anything he sets his mind to, so the sky is the limit when it comes to future careers!

There's no doubt these boys are busy, but they have something else to focus on besides their side projects—the final two movies in the Twilight series!

# CHAPTER 19
# The Boys Offstage

So what do the guys do when they aren't making movies?

Most of Jackson's spare time is taken up by his band, 100 Monkeys. So why the name? "The 'Hundredth Monkey Effect' is a really cool scientific experience," Jackson explained to MTV. "All these monkeys, they gave them sweet potatoes. And the monkeys learned themselves how to wash them in a stream to make them taste better . . . It's basically the idea of the collective consciousness. As soon as so many people have one idea or one belief, it affects the greater majority of that breed of animal, human or insect."

What does Jackson play? "Mainly guitar, keys, bass," he reported to *Portrait* magazine. "We switch it up though so I play the mandolin and the banjo too. It's mostly blues and southern rock . . . very contemporized though! It's so much fun! It's a 3 man band but we all switch instruments and we all sing. Lots of harmonies etc. . . . we just love playing together!" So what are they like to listen to? "We're basically a live band," Jackson warned *Portrait* magazine, "because we do a lot of improvs. We make up songs on the spot. All the music on our myspace is improvisations." He explained their process a bit more to *MediaBlvd* magazine, saying, "It's like a jam band, except we do sing and make up lyrics. Whenever we record, the rule is that we only get one try. You can't have a redo. You can lay one thing down and do one set of over-dubs, but that's it. We try to break it down to a simple, natural, live, creative art type of thing."

The band is doing well, performing at several local L.A. bars—and it doesn't hurt that most of the other *Twilight* cast members show up to as many of their gigs as possible! As Jackson proudly told foforks.com, "All the cast who are of legal drinking age in America have come to the show, I believe. I lucked out with an amazing on-screen family."

The year 2009 is definitely a busy one for the

100 Monkeys. As Jackson told radaronline.com back in May, "Our EP should be coming out in two or three weeks on iTunes, with three singles from our full length album, and a special surprise if you order the CD directly from us! Our full length album is set for release in the fall of this year." But of course they couldn't go about creating an album in the normal way! Jackson told teenmag.com, ". . . our band (100 Monkeys) will be focusing a lot more in terms of getting out our actual written album out there. We have an album we're in the middle of mixing and mastering right now which is a complete jam session album of all improvised music, including improvised lyrics, so everything in the song is one take, one track, you don't get a redo. It's kind of like the way Jack White produced Loretta Lynn for her album. We kind of took that idea and ran with it. We're mixing that album and hopefully will start playing out a lot more." Wow!

Does Jackson intend to give up acting for music? No, he assured *MediaBlvd* magazine, "I don't really want to focus so much on the music side of making things happen. I'm an actor, first and foremost." But that doesn't mean music isn't important to him. "I can't call it a hobby because it's so much more than that but I don't want to do music as a career," he told *Portrait*. "It's a huge part of my life though . . . I need it to survive! I would love to have a place to play! I'm also working on an album by myself but if nothing happens with it, I don't mind. It's mostly for myself." Hopefully Jackson will decide to share it with the rest of us, too!

Kellan's time off from *Twilight* is all about relaxing, hanging out, and sports, sports, sports. The more extreme, the better. "I love snowboarding," he admitted to the *Los Angeles Times* blog, "but I can't tell that to the studio because I'm not supposed to be snowboarding just before shooting [*New Moon*]." He's also been doing a lot of reading, but most of it has been work-related. "Yes, way too many in a way," he told about.com when they asked if people had been sending him more scripts since *Twilight*. "Like I feel like that's all I'm doing is reading scripts. I've read a lot of great ones, but a lot of the ones that we've been going after since, this recession's going on, a lot of movies are there and I'll read them and

I'll be hungry for them and I'll do the meetings and I'll get the parts and then it'll fall through." The other problem with reading scripts? It keeps Kellan indoors! "I'm such an outdoor freak," he admitted to about.com. "It takes up time to read and if it's something that I have to read versus like finding a good book that really captivates me, it's just that's when it starts to feel like work in a way a little bit. But I enjoy it all. I just would rather be walking my dog and I can't really walk her and read at the same time." Still, whenever he has the opportunity he's out and about and on the go, hanging out with friends, surfing, skiing, snowboarding, and just enjoying the great outdoors.

Of course, some activities are a little harder to enjoy now that he's such a celebrity. "I have so many things I enjoy in life that is out in the public," Kellan told about.com. "There's sometimes I go to local high school football games—I just love football and I love getting cheap hotdogs and just doing that experience—and it's tough going to football games now and not being able to watch any of the game and just signing shoes and paper bags, and just signing stuff." Still, he handles the attention cheerfully, and doesn't let it stop him from going out—even if he has to disguise himself to do it! Not that he has yet, but Kellan's considered it, at least. He explained to about.com, "Well I mean I love wearing hats and it's so easy. But it's funny joking around with the roommates because we have so many Halloween wigs and stuff like that. They're like, 'Oh you should do it! You should do it.' And I might do it just for fun. It hasn't gotten to the point where I feel like I have to."

Kellan enjoys other things besides sports, though. He revealed to newfaces.com, "I write a lot and have been working on some screen plays of my own, while I can. I hope to write and direct my own movie one day." Plus, he has another activity right now that he finds incredibly rewarding in a completely different way—the Royal Family Kids' Camp. "From Sunday to Friday, we throw this week-long camp, down at Point Loma University," Kellan told *MediaBlvd* magazine, "and we have these kids from group homes and kids who were molested, growing up. They have all these issues inside and they've never been loved, and they've never known who their mother or father is. A lot of times, they've never even had a birthday. And so, the last day that we're there, we throw a giant birthday for all of them, and we give them birthday presents and cupcakes and we sing 'Happy Birthday.' Seeing these kids melt down and say, 'Is this really for me?' is really heartbreaking. Having them call me daddy, I just want to take them home and give them a world that they've never had. It's gut-wrenching to say goodbye. And, a lot of times, they're crying, holding onto your leg, saying, 'I don't want to leave! I had the best time here!' There are Royal Family Kids' Camps all around the world. That's what's so amazing about it. It's not just local. There are divisions, all across the nation, as well as internationally. It's quite an amazing program, and it's very rewarding to do. I just love it. I love kids, and I love giving back." For more information about the Royal Family Kids' Camps, check out www.rfkc.org.

Robert puts most of his spare time into his music, just like Jackson. But whereas Jackson is all about horsing around onstage with his friends,

Robert prefers the solitary approach. Though he actually got the chance to perform two songs for *Twilight*! "I wrote one of the songs," he told *Los 40 Principales Spain*, "and the other one was written by a friend. Catherine heard the songs and she decided to put them in the movie, Only one of them is in the soundtrack: 'Never Think.'" Robert went on to say that he's solitary in general: "I don't go out much. I like to spend the day by myself doing my things and then socialize at night. I get bored talking to people. I ask someone out for dinner and 15 minutes later I'm tired of them." One thing Robert never gets tired of is working on his music. "I'm in talks to do a soundtrack for another movie, composing," he revealed to fandango.com. "I cannot say what it is yet, but I really, really, really want to do it. I don't think I'm going to have anything on *New Moon*, but never say never." His instrument of choice? "I love the piano. I never really had any aspirations to be an actor when I was young. I wanted to play the piano in a bar, to be the old dude with a whiskey glass, all disheveled," he told *Life & Style*. But Rob may have changed his mind since then. "I did a couple of gigs, which people filmed and put on the Internet and it kind of ruined the whole experience for me," he told thestar.com. "So I've kind of stopped now and I think I'm going to wait for all this fuss to die down before I start doing live gigs again." Still, he told *Vanity Fair*, "I play a lot of music. That's what I wanted to do before the acting thing accidentally took off—be a musician." It's unlikely Robert will give up something that means that much to him, or that it'll be too long before the thrill of playing lures him back onto the stage.

As the youngest of the four, it's no surprise that Taylor is still in school. But it may not be the school you think! "I tested out of high school and now I'm taking college classes," Taylor explained to *Vanity Fair*. Taylor can't fit a full load of college courses into his hectic schedule, but he's slowly working toward earning his bachelor's degree. His education is very important to him, especially because Taylor knows the entertainment world can be fickle. If he suddenly stops getting acting jobs, he'd like to have a solid education that he could build a different career on.

When Taylor isn't studying, he always makes it a priority to spend time catching up with his friends. Taylor has tons of friends in Michigan, Los Angeles, and all over the country because of acting and martial arts. "My favorite part of being in a movie is [that] you get to meet a lot of nice people and you get good relationships from that and it's a lot of fun to meet those new people. And it's fun playing characters not like yourself and being someone totally different for about three months," Taylor said to ultimatedisney.com. Taylor has made some amazing friends working on movies, like Taylor Dooley and Cayden Boyd from *The Adventures of Sharkboy and Lavagirl;* Alyson Stoner from *Cheaper by the Dozen 2* (Taylor plays Eliot Murtaugh, one of the eight Murtaugh children who become rivals to the Baker family); and Robert, Jackson, and Kellan from *Twilight,* of course! It's nice for Taylor to have friends who are also actors since they can understand how passionate Taylor is about his career and they can relate to all the pressures of fame. Taylor spends most of his time with them and his friends from his school in Los Angeles, but he keeps up with his other pals with lots of phone calls, e-mails, and text messages. Taylor considers himself lucky to have remained friends with lots of kids from his childhood. "Kids still looked at me as Taylor, because they knew me from before," Taylor told the *Grand Rapids Press.* "You gotta remember who your friends were before you got famous." Taylor and his friends like to get together to go to the mall or movies, hang out at a nearby beach, or play football, basketball, and baseball.

Like his costar Kellan, the only thing Taylor loves more than acting is playing sports. He plays with his friends whenever he can, but would jump at the chance to play on a team again if his schedule ever calms down. He loves baseball, basketball, and football best, but he also enjoys soccer, horseback riding, and swimming. Taylor was on his high-school football teams until he left school. "I played football my whole life and had to give it up last year because I had to miss too many practices and it was kind of rough for me. It is kind of hard watching the high school football games now. I played running back and slot receiver, and strong safety on defense," Taylor told acedmagazine.com. He misses playing, but he still finds plenty of time to watch his favorite sports! "My favorite college team is the Michigan Wolverines because I was born and raised in Michigan. And they're actually pretty good too! As for NFL, I don't really have a favorite . . . But I'm a big college fan. We watch college football a lot," Taylor told the *Oregon Herald*. You might be surprised that Taylor doesn't root for the Detroit Lions in the NFL, but recently they haven't been a very good team, so it must be difficult for Taylor—and other Michigan sports fans—to watch their team lose every year! Good thing Detroit has a pretty good team in the NBA, as Taylor explained to the *Oregon Herald*, "Well, we try to be Detroit fans, but it's really tough. We are however, big Detroit Pistons fans, who were champions last year and are in the finals this year [2005]. And I can't wait to watch them play the [San Antonio] Spurs."

Taylor hasn't competed at martial arts since he was thirteen—he decided he couldn't do both that and his acting. As he explained to *Vanity Fair*, "I gave up karate for acting, and now I'm very glad I made that choice." But he still practices. "I still try and keep up with it when I can in my free time. I go down to the XMA headquarters in North Hollywood where my Karate trainer just opened up this big complex and it's awesome. It's topnotch," Taylor told about.com. Taylor also used to dance with hip-hop and jazz dance groups, but he gave that up around the same time that he quit karate, and for the same reasons. "Dancing—I don't really do any more because I'm way too busy," Taylor said to ultimatedisney.com. Taylor has had to give up a lot of his favorite hobbies for his career, but you won't hear him complaining about it. He loves acting and he loves his fans. But, when he's not working, Taylor takes every chance he can get to have fun with his old pastimes!

Taylor and his family also go back to Michigan on a regular basis—and when they're there, Taylor can drive to see his old friends! Being able to drive was his favorite thing about turning sixteen right before he started filming *Twilight*. He had to drive in a few scenes in the movie, so he practiced as much as he could to make sure he was ready. "Yeah. I've got my license in my back pocket to show them I'm ok and that I won't kill them . . . hopefully. *[He laughs.]* I'm going to test out driving Bella's truck [from the Twilight movies] and my family's truck. One of them is an automatic, so that will be nice and easy. The other one has no power steering, so I'll have to muscle it. That will be interesting. I've never done that before," Taylor told MTV.com. Taylor got to drive a truck while he was on the set, which was really fun for the new driver! "Yeah. It's really old and beat-up, and that's the one without the power steering. So I'm going to be driving with my [real-life] dad right next to me, and that should be interesting. We want to make sure I get used to it, so it looks natural," Taylor continued to MTV.com. Of course, now Taylor is a driving expert, and he has really enjoyed having the freedom to go wherever he wants without having to ask his mom or dad for a lift! When Taylor finally does get his own car, it will probably be blue. "My favorite color is baby blue. Like royal blue, baby blue, that kind of thing," Taylor said to ultimatedisney.com. One thing's for sure—it looks like nothing but blue skies ahead for these guys and their careers!

# CHAPTER 20
## Girls, Girls, Girls

Jackson, Kellan, Robert, and Taylor are all total hotties, so it's no surprise that girls everywhere are falling for them. So what is their dating status, anyway? Well, not surprisingly, it's complicated. Technically all four are currently single—at least, that's what each of them claims. But is that really the case?

Jackson's expressed interest in his *Twilight* costar Ashley Greene, who plays his on-screen love interest Alice Cullen—and vice versa! "He and I both don't have time to date, but we do have amazing chemistry," Ashley told the *Herald-Sun*. "We both have such big crushes on each other and it clearly shows. We got along instantly and the day we met, he was teaching me how to swing dance. He (Rathbone) does everything. He sings, he dances, and he's so sweet. Even my mum has a crush on him and tells me, 'You should date him.' So, who knows, maybe when we both stop running around the world." In the meantime, Jackson claims his only girlfriend is his guitar, Annabelle— "She's beautiful, but shy," he revealed to *Vanity Fair*. What sort of girl is Jackson interested in, though? "A girl who knows what she wants," he told jackson-rathbone.org, "and has a drive in life. Definitely a girl who is artistically inclined, musicality a plus. I'm very southern in my dating habits."

Kellan was dating someone, but they broke up shortly before *Twilight* was released. In an interview with twilightcocoa.blogspot.com, Kellan said, "I am single now. Um, yeah. I should say, 'Yes I'm single YEA!'" He did clarify, however, that it was "a great break up. It really was a very loving break up. I have never really had a break up like this. But you know we have different lives. Things change. It was very mutual. Things got really complicated, but we are still good friends. It's interesting being single because I haven't been single in forever. It's kind of nice."

Since then Kellan has been described as dating costar Ashley Greene (though it seems like her heart's taken by Jackson!), Disney star Selena Gomez, Lindsay Lohan, and most recently with *90210* costar AnnaLynne McCord, but Kellan himself just laughs and says they're all false rumors. "It's funny, I heard I'm dating [AnnaLynne]," he said to eonline.com. "It's all news to me. I always open up the magazines, and I'm like, 'Wow, I have a new girlfriend.' I'm quite single; I'm happy being single." If he was dating, what sort of girl would attract Kellan's interest? He told twilightcocoa.blogspot.com, "If I was on the market looking for someone special again—I want someone who can laugh and have fun. Someone who can be in their pajamas, watch TV and have a good time. I really don't like the complicated girls. The more easy going ones are my favorite."

Robert is dating costar and on-screen love interest Kristen Stewart—at least, that's what most of the celebrity gossip magazines say! They've even coined a name for the couple: "Robsten." But is it real or as fictional as Edward and Bella's relationship? The latter, according to Robert. He told *ET,* "It becomes a joke. There was some magazine the other day about me and Kristen and when you look at it and realize it's on the front of a magazine. You realize that people are actually reading that even though how ridiculous it is. It's really bizarre." At least one site has claimed that Robert was actually seeing Nikki Reed, who plays on-screen sis Rosalie Hale, during the filming of both *Twilight* and *New Moon*. Robert claims that isn't the case, however—and so does Nikki's on-screen love interest, Kellan! "I think I would have more rumors saying I'm dating Nikki [Reed] than Rob because Nikki and I hang out a lot," Kellan told eonline.com. "I would love to see the next girlfriend that Rob has or a girlfriend that he would have. So those rumors are false." Then there are the rumors that Robert's dating a Brazilian model, or actress Camilla Belle, who's been seen around town with Joe Jonas. Are any of these true? Robert says no. "I don't see people," he told people.com. "I don't even have people's phone numbers. I almost don't want to have a girlfriend in this environment."

Robert also worries about how any girl he does date will handle his celebrity status. As he told *Pantalla Semanal* magazine, "Obviously if I go out with a girl, she'll get pulled into the fame thing. In fact, even some of my ex girlfriends have been questioned. It's crazy, but when I'll go out with someone, that person will be introduced to a life that she won't necessarily care for. That's preoccupying. I think that any girl who isn't part of this world would be scared." Still, there are bound to be a lot of girls who would be happy to make such a sacrifice!

As for Taylor, he's got some romance of his own going on, according to the tabloids. He and singer-actress Selena Gomez have been seen hanging out together a lot. They've both been working on films in Vancouver, him on *New Moon* and her on *Ramona and Beezus* (adapted from the classic Beverly Cleary children's book). They've been dubbed "Taylena" by the media. Are they really a couple, though, or just good friends? "She's a great girl. A great friend," Taylor told *Access Hollywood*. "I hope I'm not breaking [the fans'] hearts. She's a great girl." Well, that sounds nice—but confusing! But Selena recently wrote on her blog, "I remember when i was 12 telling my friends i would never ever wear dresses because i thought they were too prissy.

Now I own more floral dresses than pants. Or how i hated mustard and gagged at the sight of it, now I will not touch a hotdog without it. I also said that I would never fall in love until i was much older to really understand the word." Is Selena saying she's fallen in love with someone? If so, the obvious choice is Taylor—they've certainly been spending enough time together! And according to *Life & Style*, the two had dinner together on May 4, 2009, and "Taylor walked Selena back to her hotel afterward," a witness told them. "When she didn't think anyone was around, she wrapped her arms around his neck and gave him a big kiss!" That certainly sounds like they're together! The couple has one major obstacle, though, besides the usual issues of fame and public life—and that's Taylor's dad! "My dad says I can't date until I'm 28," Taylor told starpulse.com. "I'm definitely hoping to negotiate that one down." He understands why, though. "I realized that my parents were strict to make sure that I didn't get a big head, and that's a good thing," he continued. "My parents brought me up to have respect and not take things for granted." Taylor might be taken, but it looks like Jackson, Robert, and Kellan are still on the market! Who knows—maybe you'll get the chance to meet—and woo—a *Twilight* boy someday!

# CHAPTER 21
# Fun Facts

Think you know all about the *Twilight* boys? Well, here are some fun facts you may have missed!

## Jackson Rathbone

**Full name:** Monroe Jackson Rathbone V
**Birthdate:** December 21, 1984
**Birthplace:** Singapore
**Height:** 5'8"
**Hair:** Light brown
**Eyes:** Blue
**Nicknames:** J. Action, Jay
**Siblings:** Three sisters (two older and one younger)
**Pets:** A cat named Dean
**Has lived in:** Indonesia (Maydan & Jakarta), Texas (Midland), Los Angeles,

northwestern Michigan, Toronto, London, Norway, Connecticut

**Interests:** Watching/studying movies, listening to music, playing music, directing

**Favorite movies:** *Seven Samurai; Dead Man* (Lars Von Trier's documentary on directing), *The Five Obstructions*

**Favorite music:** Robert Johnson, John Lee Hooker, Steppin' In It, Wilco, Modest Mouse, Kasier Chiefs, Sigur Ros, Mogwai, Nina Simone, The Shins, Clap Your Hands Say Yeah, Chet Baker, Spencer Bell, Lou Reed, The Kinks, Tom Waits, Man Man, David Bowie, Frank Sinatra, Dean Martin, Sammy Davis Jr., The Stevedores, and TV on the Radio

**Favorite sports:** Baseball, track, basketball, soccer, football

**Favorite football team:** Dallas Cowboys

**Favorite TV shows:** *Dexter, It's Always Sunny in Philadelphia, Mad Men, South Park*

**Celebrity crushes:** January Jones and
   Bryce Dallas Howard
**Personal hero:** Johnny Depp

Jackson once ran a mobile DJ business.

As an acting major, he flourished in Shakespearian plays.

He isn't big on sweets, but loves Texas-style barbecue.

He is very down-to-earth and close with his family.

He's happy to spend quiet evenings at home writing and playing music with his friends.

Jackson was roommates with actor/singer Alex Boyd.

He is roommates with actor and fellow 100 Monkeys member Ben Graupner.

He considers Michael Jackson's "Thriller" a classic.

He wasn't allowed to watch horror flicks growing up, so when a friend gave him a box set of the George A.

Romero classics *Night of the Living Dead, Dawn of the Dead*, and *Day of the Dead*, Jackson had to hide them beneath his bed.

He was on *Disney 411* as a reporter.

He went to Interlochen, a private school for the arts in Michigan.

His theater credits include lead roles in *A Midsummer's Night Dream, Macbeth, Les Miserables, Grease, Jesus Christ Superstar*, and *The Lion, the Witch, and the Wardrobe.*

He has worked with actor Clint Howard twice, first in *River's End* and second in *Senior Skip Day.*

He can play the harmonica and guitar like one of his musical inspirations, Bob Dylan.

He learned to play baseball left-handed for his role in *Twilight.*

He was taught how to box by his father after getting into a fight with a kid in elementary school on picture day.

He once had an ear piercing at the age of sixteen, and a tongue piercing at eighteen. Both are gone now.

He has one tattoo.

After having to learn how to play the guitar for the role of "Doody" in *Grease*, Jackson was inspired to continue playing.

He is terrified of spiders.

He is colorblind.

He is not a fan of sushi, but ate it anyway for Ashley Greene's twenty-first birthday.

He would like to work with Clint Eastwood one day.

His dad wanted to name him "Paul" instead of Monroe Jackson.

# Kellan Lutz

**Full name:** Kellan Christopher Lutz
**Birthdate:** March 15, 1985
**Birthplace:** Dickinson, North Dakota
**Hair:** Blond
**Eyes:** Blue
**Height:** 6'1"
**Siblings:** Six brothers and one sister (Kellan is in the middle)
**Nickname:** Krazy Kellan
**Shoe size:** 12
**Role models:** His mom, Robert Redford, Leonardo DiCaprio
**Pet:** A dog named Kola
**Favorite sports:** Football, boxing, skateboarding, track, baseball, basketball, lacrosse, swimming, tennis, racquetball, badminton, skiing, snowboarding
**Favorite books:** *Wild at Heart, The Purpose-Driven Life, The Color Purple.*

He is also a fan of John Grisham's books.

**Favorite band:** Incubus

**Favorite song:** "Salvation" by Citizen Cope

**Favorite musical acts:** Modest Mouse, Citizen Cope, 2-pac, Blue Man Group, Blue October, Chevelle, Coheed and Cambria, Damian Marley, Dilated Peoples, God Lives Underwater, Incubus, Jack Johnson, Lupe Fiasco, Matisyahu, Nickelback, OneRepublic, Orgy, A Perfect Circle, The Postal Service, The Red Hot Chili Peppers, The Red Jumpsuit Apparatus, Until June

**Favorite cause:** Boys and Girls Club and Royal Family Kids' Camp

**Favorite gadget:** His Microsoft Zune

**Favorite sports team:** Phoenix Suns

**Favorite website:** addictinggames.com

**Favorite place:** South Africa

**Favorite color:** Neon green

**Favorite fruit:** Strawberries

**Favorite ice cream:** Strawberry, specifically from Cold Stone Creamery

**Favorite fast food:** Taco Bell

**Favorite designer:** James Perse
**Favorite breakfast:** Cinnamon Toast
   Crunch, with some good old steak
   and eggs
**Celebrity crush:** Jessica Biel
**Favorite actor:** Robert Redford
**Favorite movies:** *Fight Club* and *Spy Game*
**Favorite TV show:** *Lost*
**Personal motto:** In life never stop
   dreaming . . . For in dreams, we
   never stop living.

Kellan intended on keeping his natural curly hair for the role of Emmett Cullen, but had recently had a buzz cut for a different film and his hair didn't grow fast enough for the filming of *Twilight*.

The most embarrassing place his phone ever began ringing was during a church baptism. His ringtone was Sir Mix-A Lot's "Baby Got Back." The volume was on high and it took him at least fifteen seconds to turn the ringer off.

Prior to being cast as Emmett Cullen in *Twilight*, he

was an Abercrombie & Fitch model.

According to Kellan, he and Peter Facinelli would play pranks on the *Twilight* cast and crew.

To "buff up" for *Twilight*, Kellan ate a lot of protein. He actually eats sixteen eggs for breakfast.

Kellan loves the Nintendo Wii. He once played a two-hour tennis game against his brother on "Wii Sports."

If Kellan had to choose between a Blackberry, Sidekick, or Treo, he would choose a Treo.

Before breaking into acting, Kellan attended Orange County's Chapman University for chemical engineering.

According to Kellan, his worst quality is his competitiveness and his best quality is how easygoing and fun-loving he is.

Kellan can speak fluent Spanish.

Kellan says he was a "mamma's boy" growing up.

Kellan lives in California with his four roommates.

Kellan keeps a jar of smooth peanut butter on his bedside table that he eats in the middle of the night.

He did his own stunts in *Deep Winter* and had a great time doing it.

# Robert Pattinson

**Full name:** Robert Thomas Pattinson
**Birthdate:** May 13, 1986
**Birthplace:** London
**Height:** 6'1"
**Eyes:** Bluish gray
**Hair:** Brownish blond
**Siblings:** Two sisters, Lizzie and Victoria
**Nicknames:** Rpatzz, Spunk Ransom
**Favorite actors:** Jack Nicholson, Michael Gambon, Warwick Davis, Al Pacino
**Favorite restaurant:** In-N-Out Burger
**Favorite superheroes:** Spider-Man and *X-Men's* Gambit
**Favorite cartoons:** *Sharkey & George* and *Hammertime*
**Favorite movie vampires:** Max Schreck's *Nosferatu*; Gary Oldman's *Dracula*

Up until he was twelve, Pattinson's sisters dressed him up as a girl and introduced him as Claudia.

His Dad wanted him to be an actor.

Twelve was a turning point for Robert—he moved to a coed school and became "cool" with the discovery of hair gel.

He started acting at age fifteen in plays.

He cut his acting teeth with the Barnes Theatre Company in heavy numbers like Shakespeare's *Macbeth* and Hardy's *Tess of the D'Urbervilles*.

His first film role was Giselher in *Ring of the Nibelungs*, quickly followed by the role of older Rawdy Crawley in *Vanity Fair*.

He aspires to be like Jack Nicholson.

He enjoys music and is an excellent musician, playing the guitar and keyboard.

He attended Harrodian private school in London with fellow actor and good friend Tom Sturridge.

He was expelled from school when he was twelve.

His fashion sense is inspired by James Dean.

For the role of Edward Cullen, Robert flew from England to director Catherine Hardwicke's house to audition. There, he and Kristen Stewart, who was already cast as Bella Swan, rehearsed the "Love Scene"/"Meadow Scene" on Hardwicke's own bed.

He did a paper round for £10 ($20) a week when he was ten years old.

He was obsessed with earning money until he turned fifteen.

He was in a band named Bad Girl that played "rocky stuff."

He says he doesn't want to be paid ever again and wants to do everything for free—can we have that in writing?

He says he is determined to take on really weird roles following his parts in *Harry Potter* and *Twilight*.

One of his first roles was a small part as a Cuban dancer.

He played a World War II pilot in a BBC2 play—

*The Haunting of Toby Jugg.*

He used to throw up on the set of *Harry Potter* because of his nerves.

He directed a play once.

He employed a personal trainer after a costume designer said his body looked like he should be playing a "sissy" or something.

He was not a *Harry Potter* fan nor had he read any of the books before getting his part as Cedric.

He had nightmares about his *Harry Potter* premiere for months before it happened.

He was named "British Star of Tomorrow" by *Times Online* in 2005.

He would have liked the role of *Harry Potter*.

He learned to scuba dive for his *Harry Potter* role.

He asked Michael Gambon for his autograph.

Someone once stole his laces from his shoes. He now wears shoes without laces as a sort of signature!

He says he is no good at accents.

He has appeared in an advertising campaign for Hacketts (an upscale London men's outfitters).

Robert has a thriving Spanish website.

His shirtless scenes in *Twilight* have been scrapped because he "looked weird."

He got bags of angry letters saying he should not play Edward in *Twilight*.

Robert became known to his fans as "Spunk Ransom" after admitting he disliked his name. "I hate any reference to my name," he told MTV. "I wish people would just completely invent a new one." Spunk Ransom was Pattinson's suggested alternative.

Robert, who plays piano and guitar, has two songs featured in *Twilight*. "I cried the first time I heard the two songs," director Catherine Hardwicke told MTV. "They're deep; they're very soulful."

While filming *Twilight*, Robert injured himself on his very first shot. "I wasn't even doing a stunt. I was just trying to pick up Kristen Stewart and I almost tore my hamstring because I hadn't been doing enough squats," the actor told the *Los Angeles Times*. "It was very embarrassing."

While on the *Twilight* set, an enthusiastic fan asked a crewmember to bring her baby on the set and have Robert take a photo with the child. "So there's a photo of me like biting a baby's head," he said.

# Taylor Lautner

**Full name:** Taylor Daniel Lautner
**Birthdate:** February 11, 1992
**Birthplace:** Grand Rapids, Michigan
**Height:** 5'9"
**Hair:** Black
**Eyes:** Brown
**Siblings:** One sister, Makena
**Pet:** A Maltese named Roxy
**Favorite actors:** Tom Cruise and Mike Meyers
**Favorite actress:** Jessica Simpson
**Favorite color:** Baby blue
**Favorite food:** Steak
**Favorite ice cream flavor:** Cake batter
**Favorite martial artist:** Mike Chat
**Favorite method for relaxing:** Playing video games at a friend's house
**Favorite movie:** *Accepted, Braveheart*
**Favorite music artist:** Outkast, Black Eyed Peas

**Favorite types of food:** Mexican and Chinese

**Favorite TV shows:** *American Idol, The Contender*, UFC, *The Apprentice*

**Favorite shoes:** Vans

**Favorite sports:** Football and baseball

**Favorite sports teams:** Texas Longhorns and Michigan Wolverines

Taylor does, indeed, have a cell phone. It's a Nokia and his plan is Sprint.

He enjoys playing football, baseball, and basketball.

He has made a music video for the song "Apologize," which is available to see on his MySpace page.

He owns a PS2.

He smiles frequently.

He hangs out with stars such as Alyson Stoner, Taylor Dooley, Victoria Justice, and Jenna Boyd.

He wears a wig for his role in *Twilight*.

He is of French, Dutch, German, and Native American descent.

Taylor is a mostly A student with an occasional A-.

In the past he had to stay up until 10:30 or 11 o'clock to finish his homework.

Taylor trains in karate three or four times a week.

He became interested in martial arts when he was six years old.

Taylor calls himself a dork!

His two best friends are a dancer and a magician.

Taylor says he can't skateboard because he'd hurt himself!

Taylor's favorite thing about working on the movie *Twilight* is the fans.

He wants to be a director and screenwriter, as well as continue his acting career.

He had to get used to pushing a wheelchair for the movie *Twilight*, so it would look like he had been doing it all his life.

He's a keen martial artist who, from the age of seven, has won many karate tournaments on a local, national, and international level.

He received his driver's license in 2008.

Taylor played football during freshman year in high school.

He had to start training the day after *Twilight* was finished for his role of Jacob Black in *New Moon*. He gained thirty pounds of muscle for the expanded role!

# CHAPTER 22

# Supernatural Boys Quiz

Jackson, Kellan, Robert, and Taylor are all friends, but they're all very different. Each of the four has different interests, different hobbies, and a completely different personality. So which one appeals to you the most? Which of the four would you get along with best? Let's find out!

1) It's Saturday, the sun is out, and you have the day off! What do you want to do with your free time?

   **A.** Gather some friends, grab your instruments, and jam!

   **B.** Hit the slopes or the beach, whichever's closer!

   **C.** Play a little basketball or maybe work on a song.

**D.** Head down to the dojo or out to the football field.

2) You've been cast in a movie! It's not a big part, but it's exciting nonetheless. What do you do on your first day?

    **A.** Get to know people, relax, and hang out.

    **B.** Goof off, tell jokes, and make friends.

    **C.** Study your lines until you have them memorized.

    **D.** Watch everyone else and take mental notes.

3) You're hanging out with some friends and you wind up at a karaoke bar. What do you do?

    **A.** Jump up onstage, haul your friends up with you, and start playing something—never mind the karaoke, you have instruments and mics!

    **B.** Pick a silly song and completely ham it up.

    **C.** Find a song you actually know well, and give the performance your all.

**D.** Let your friends talk you into singing, then quickly give the mic back and return to watching and laughing and egging the rest of them on.

4) You've been offered a role in a movie, but you're going to have to wear a wig for it. What do you say?

   **A.** Heck yes! You love putting on disguises and dressing up and becoming someone else!

   **B.** Sure, if that's what the director wants, why not?

   **C.** If you have to, but isn't there some way to avoid it?

   **D.** You'll wear it, of course, but you aren't happy about it.

## If you chose . . .

Mostly As—You're a fun-loving free spirit, and you're all about music and laughter and friends. So is Jackson Rathbone! He's the most energetic of the

*Twilight* boys, and one of the most light-hearted. He also loves to play different roles and change his appearance for each new movie.

Mostly Bs—Kellan Lutz is the joker of the group, and the extreme sportsman. He loves to surf and ski, and he'll try any other extreme sport as well. He's also very easygoing, a lot of fun, and always quick to joke with his friends. It sounds like the two of you would get along fine!

Mostly Cs—Robert Pattinson is the most soulful of the group. He's a musician but he takes his music very seriously, just like his acting. He puts his full effort and concentration into everything he does. Sound intense—or just dreamy?

Mostly Ds—You're quiet, careful, a little studious without being too bookish, a little athletic without being overzealous, willing to do what you're told and happy just to hang out with your friends. So is Taylor Lautner! You two have a lot in common!

# CHAPTER 23

# Finding the Boys Online

Jackson, Robert, Kellan, and Taylor are rising young stars, which means almost every week brings a new article or interview or photo of one or more of them! The good news is, the Internet makes it easy to keep up with them and read all about their latest roles, appearances, and activities. Below are a list of websites to help you find out more about each and every one of the boys of *Twilight*.

But always be careful online, and never give out any sort of personal information—like your name, address, phone number, or the name of your school or sports team—and never try to meet someone in person that you met online. And when you are surfing the net, you have to remember that not everything you read there is true. There are lots of people creating websites out there, and sometimes they create false information to make their sites more exciting. For example, neither Jackson nor Kellan have MySpace pages, even though plenty of MySpace pages claim to be theirs. So never assume something is true because you read it online. And remember, never surf the Web without your parents' permission. Can't find your favorite website? Websites come and go, so don't worry—there's sure to be another site to replace it soon!

**www.twilightthemovie.com**

This is the official website for *Twilight,* the movie. It has cool interviews with the cast, wallpapers, IM icons, widgets, and tons of other exclusive *Twilight* content.

**www.stepheniemeyer.com**

The official website of Stephenie Meyer, author of the Twilight series.

**www.thetwilightsaga.com**

This is a great fansite for the Twilight saga.

**www.myspace.com/these100monkeys**

This is Jackson's band's official MySpace page.

**www.jackson-rathbone.com**

Jackson doesn't have a site himself, but this is one of the best of the fan websites.

**www.jackson-rathbone.org**

This is another excellent fan-run page for Jackson info.

**www.kellanlutz.com**

Kellan's official website. He doesn't update it often, however.

**www.kellanlutzonline.com**

A great Kellan Lutz fansite that keeps you posted on all the latest Kellan news.

**robertpattinson.org**

A really good Robert Pattinson fansite.

**www.robertpattinsononline.com**

Another excellent Robert Pattinson site.

**www.taylor-lautner.com**

A really great Taylor fansite.

**taylorlautner.info**

Another rockin' fansite with lots of wallpapers, pictures, and tons of Taylor updates!